The Image-Is-Everything Presidency

Dilemmas in American Politics

Series Editor   **L. Sandy Maisel,** *Colby College*

Dilemmas in American Politics offers teachers and students a series of quality books on timely topics and key institutions in American government. Each text will examine a "real world" dilemma and will be structured to cover the historical, theoretical, policy relevant, and future dimensions of its subject.

BOOKS IN THIS SERIES

· ·

The Image-Is-Everything Presidency

Dilemmas in American Leadership

Richard W. Waterman
University of New Mexico

Robert Wright
University of New Mexico

Gilbert St. Clair
College of Santa Fe

Westview Press
A Member of the Perseus Books Group

Dilemmas in American Politics

Copyright © 1999 by Westview Press, A Member of the Perseus Books Group

Published in 1999 in the United States of America by Westview Press, 5500 Central Avenue, Boulder,
Colorado 80301-2877, and in the United Kingdom by Westview Press, 12 Hid's Copse Road, Cumnor
Hill, Oxford OX2 9JJ

Library of Congress Cataloging-in-Publication Data
Waterman, Richard W.
   The image-is-everything presidency : dilemmas in American
leadership / by Richard W. Waterman, Robert Wright, and Gilbert St. Clair.
      p.   cm.
   Includes bibliographical references (p.   ) and index.
   ISBN 0-8133-6891-X (hc). — ISBN 0-8133-6892-8 (pbk)
   1. Presidents—United States.   2. Public relations and politics—
United States.   I. St. Clair, Gilbert K.   II. Wright, Robert
(Robert Lee).   III. Title.
JK518.W383   1999
352.23'2748'0973—dc21   98-52006
                                                                        CIP

The paper used in this publication meets the requirements of the American National Standard for
Permanence of Paper for Printed Library Materials Z39.48-1984.

10   9   8   7   6   5   4   3   2

*We dedicate our book to Chester A. Arthur,
because we doubt that anyone else ever has.*

Contents

Tables and Illustrations

Tables

Illustrations

Preface

When we first began this project we had no idea that we would be writing in the midst of a major presidential scandal. While Bill Clinton was under investigation almost from the beginning of his presidency, the idea that we would be writing about the presidential image during a period in which the impeachment of the sitting president was a real possibility never entered our minds. We had decided to make this book as topical as possible, so we continuously updated the book as we went along, in fact to the very last possible moment, to try to cover all of the details of the emerging presidential scandal. As we wrote, the Starr Report was before the public, and the House Judiciary Committee had voted two articles of impeachment. The president's job approval ratings remained in the 60 percent range, and only about one-third of various poll respondents indicated that they wanted the president to resign or be impeached. On the other hand, major newspapers and politicians (including many Democrats) called for the president's resignation and, while the president dug in his heels for the fight of his political life, conventional wisdom was that he would survive. In short, these are certainly interesting times to be writing a book about the presidency.

From the perspective of the book, which focuses on presidential images, it is also fortuitous. We have seen a president's reputation and image change dramatically over time. At first Bill Clinton was seen as a traditional politician, which today is a political kiss of death. During the 1992 campaign his image was then reformulated into a kinder, gentler candidate: playing the saxophone on a late-night television talk show, discussing on MTV whether he wore boxers or briefs. While this new image helped to get him elected, in subsequent months, the public and political pundits began to perceive the president in a new way: as not quite up to the job. The spectre of a failed presidency loomed ahead. What did Clinton do? He brought Dick Morris, his former political consultant, to the White House to do an image makeover. The new image of the president as "father figure," espousing a positive moral agenda and portraying the president as more presidential-looking, worked. Clinton was reelected in 1996. But the scandal involving a young White House intern raised yet a new image of the president. Clinton had never been able to totally distance himself from his traditional politician image—being popularly known as "Slick Willie." But when he admitted to receiving oral sex in the White House, allegedly on three occasions while talking to members of Congress on the phone, and later saying that receiving oral sex did not constitute having sexual relations, another image of the president began to develop: "Sick Willie." The president's womanizing seemed to be out of control. Ordinary Americans began to say, "the president needs help," but they were not echoing the Brownlow Committee's recommendations (proposed in 1937 during Franklin D. Roosevelt's presidency but for different reasons). They were suggesting the president needed psychological or spiritual counseling, or both. As the scandal proceeded it became apparent that Bill Clinton had clearly lost control of his image. Yet another presidency was imperiled. In sum, what is wrong with presidents and the presidency today?

In this book we provide an answer to this question. We argue that image has come to dominate our political system, particularly with regard to the presidency, and that as a result, policy substance has become less important, clearly to the detriment of presidential governing. Presidents, in fact, now choose the issues upon which they will govern in order to promote a desired personal image, as Clinton did in the 1996 presidential election. The end result, we argue, is that image has become everything and issues have become secondary matters.

Our examination of the image-is-everything presidency presents two basic types of image: historical and personal. We analyze different historical images over time to demonstrate that the presidency has always been associated with images, that image politics is certainly not new. But we argue that it has become more important over time and that, as it has, policy substance has been devalued. The metaphor that we use for this is: Presidents have put the public relations cart before the policy horse. While exceptions to this trend can clearly be identified—the Reagan Revolution of 1981 and 1982 and even the more substantive approach of Bill Clinton's first year or so in office—we see this as a problem that has evolved since at least the presidency of Richard Nixon. Presidents have not only become more interested in their personal images, they have hired public relations teams to sell these images and institutionalized public relations inside the White House. Presidents are speaking more often, generally to small, specialized audiences, but are saying less of substance. They have created sophisticated mechanisms for controlling or at least influencing the media. Perhaps most pernicious of all, presidents now seem to be perpetually running for office. Bill Clinton's 1996 reelection campaign began the day he was inaugurated as president in 1993, if not before. Presidential campaigns have thus become constant events.

Our view of the presidency and where it is headed is decidedly pessimistic. And while we do not expect everyone to agree with our thesis, we do hope that it will encourage debate and discussion. Certainly, we hope that we can elevate the role of image politics to a more prominent place in discussions of the presidency.

In writing this book we have many people we wish to thank. First, we would like to thank our respective families for their support. We would also like to thank the Department of Political Science at the University of New Mexico. Our colleagues here have provided us much intellectual support for our ideas. We are also indebted to the University of New Mexico's Institute for Public Policy, whose data from two recent surveys they conducted about the expectations gap and perceptions of the presidency of John Kennedy we have cited. We would also like to thank the reviewers of this book, Samuel Hoff of Delaware State University, James King of the University of Wyoming, and two anonymous reviewers. Their comments and suggestions are reflected on virtually every page of this book. We would also like to thank Sandy Maisel, Leo Wiegman, Kristin Milavec, and our copy editor, Jean D. Erler, of Westview Press. Their comments and suggestions also greatly helped us improve the book. Of course, as is standard practice, we admit that all errors are the responsibility of the authors, though since this is a book on the presidency, we can always try to blame any errors on the incumbent president.

Richard W. Waterman
Robert Wright
Gilbert St. Clair

The Image-Is-Everything Presidency

1

Public Expectations and Presidential Image

Image is everything.

—Andre Agassi, tennis star,
for a Nike footwear advertisement

ONE OF THE MOST FAMOUS OF THE LEGENDS OF THE LIFE
OF WASHINGTON:
THE YOUNG WASHINGTON AND THE CHERRY TREE,
Illustrated From the Story Which Gained Fame From Parson Weems's
Life of Washington.

George Washington (1732–1799), first president of the United States, shown as a young boy telling his father that he had chopped down a cherry tree. Photo courtesy of Archive Photos, reprinted with permission.

In 1961 historian Daniel Boorstin noted that the public's expectations about American society have become excessive, contradictory, and, ultimately, unrealistic. In a book titled *The Image,* Boorstin (1961: 4) described the public's expectations:

> We expect everybody to feel free to disagree, yet we expect everybody to be loyal, not to rock the boat or take the Fifth Amendment. We expect everybody to believe deeply in religion, yet not to think less of others for not believing. We expect our nation to be strong and great and vast and varied and prepared for every challenge; yet we expect our "national purpose" to be clear and simple, something that gives direction to the lives of nearly two hundred million people and yet can be bought in paperback at the corner drugstore for a dollar.

Boorstin believed that because we harbor and nourish ever more contradictory and unrealistic expectations of our society, expectations that can never be adequately fulfilled, we are forced to create "illusions with which we deceive ourselves" into thinking that our expectations have been satisfied. We create illusions and then "become so accustomed" to them "that we mistake them for reality." We then "demand that there be always more" illusions, each "bigger and better and more vivid" than the ones that came before. Boorstin concluded that these illusions "are the world of our making: the world of the image. . . . We are haunted, not by reality, but by those images we have put in place of reality" (ibid., 1961: 5–6).

Boorstin was describing American society in general, but he might as well have been describing the state of the modern presidency. Many presidential scholars and political pundits believe that public expectations of the presidency are excessive, contradictory, and unrealistic. They also argue that because the public's expectations are so unrealistic, the presidency itself is imperiled, if not outright doomed to failure. Presidential scholars have therefore asked: How can presidents satisfy these excessive, contradictory, and unrealistic expectations? We provide an answer to that question in this book, but the answer is not necessarily comforting. We will argue that successful presidents deal with such expectations in much the same way Boorstin stated Americans in general deal with their unrealistic expectations of our society; that is, they seek to create desirable illusions and images. If presidents cannot actually satisfy our unrealistic expectations, then at least they can create images that lead us to believe that they have. Through the use of carefully constructed, poll-tested images, the most successful of our recent presidents have been particularly effective at creating illusions and images of presidential leadership. We call this presidential leadership strategy the **image-is-everything presidency.**

As we shall argue throughout this book, the central dilemma for the American presidency is that the development of the image-is-everything presidency has put the public relations cart before the policy horse. The end result: an image-driven presidency in which policies are often mere props for presidents and their image makers. Substance has been devalued and replaced with symbolism and style. In the process, the world of the image maker has become increasingly confused with reality.

The Expectations Gap

In arguably the most influential book written on the subject of presidential power, Richard Neustadt (1980: 7) wrote that the public has come to believe that "the man inside the White House [can] do something about everything." For example, the "public's expectations of the president in the area of policy are substantial and include his ensuring peace, prosperity, and security" (Edwards and Wayne 1997: 99). The public also expects the president to be "a competent manager of the machinery of government; . . . a skilled engineer of the economy of the nation, . . . [and] a faithful representative of the opinion of the people" (Brownlow 1969: 35). Indeed, one of the most important political trends of the modern presidency has been "the growth in public expectations of the presidency and the expanding scope of presidential action" (Seligman and Baer 1969: 18).

The expectations gap thesis—the idea that there is a gap between what the public expects of its presidents and what presidents actually can accomplish—has been a mainstay of the presidential literature for more than thirty years. So commonly has the theory been cited that arguments for it can be found in most major works on the presidency. For example, in 1969 Louis Brownlow, who in 1937 had been the head of President Franklin Roosevelt's Committee on Administrative Management, wrote, "The nation expects more of the President than he can possibly do, more than we give him either the authority or the means to do. Thus, expecting from him the impossible, inevitably we shall be disappointed in his performance" (1969: 35). Since the 1960s this theme has been repeated with regularity by many top scholars of the presidency (for example, Cronin 1974, 1977; Moe 1985; Greenstein 1988; Genovese 1995; Edwards and Wayne 1997; Buchanan

1978; Light 1983; Hinckley 1985, 1990; Kinder 1986; Nelson 1988; Seligman and Covington 1989).

Survey research also indicates that the public has extraordinary expectations about our presidents. For example, in one of the most comprehensive empirical studies conducted to date about the public's expectations of the presidency, George Edwards, in 1983, concluded that the public expects "successful policies from the White House." Edwards compared the results of two polls, the first conducted in December 1976, the other in December 1980. The polls examined public expectations of presidents-elect (presidents elected but not yet inaugurated) Jimmy Carter and Ronald Reagan. Of the poll's respondents, 72 percent expected President-elect Carter to reduce unemployment, while 69 percent expected the same from President-elect Reagan. In other areas, 59 and 70 percent, respectively, expected each new president to reduce the cost of government; 81 and 89 percent expected him to increase government efficiency; 79 and 77 percent expected him to deal effectively with foreign policy; and 81 and 76 percent expected him to strengthen national defense. In the last area, one can of course argue that reducing the cost of government and strengthening national defense are contradictory objectives; at a minimum, it is difficult to accomplish both goals simultaneously. Yet the public clearly expected both Presidents-elect Carter and Reagan to achieve these and many other goals. To fail to do so would have been to fail to live up to the public's expectations; and all this before either man had served even one day as president of the United States!

In regard to general expectations of presidents, Edwards also noted that 82 percent of the respondents to a fall 1979 Gallup poll believed intelligence in a president to be important. When asked what other qualities were important, 81 percent identified sound judgment in a crisis; 74 percent, competence and an ability to get the job done; 66 percent, high ethical standards; 50 percent, a sense of humor; 42 percent, imagination; and 33 percent personal charm, style, and charisma. The same Gallup poll showed that the public had high expectations of the president's private behavior. Of the poll's respondents, 70 percent said they would strongly object "if the president smoked marijuana occasionally"; 43 percent, "if he told ethnic or racial jokes in private"; 38 percent, if he were not a church member; 36 percent, "if he used tranquilizers occasionally"; 33 percent, "if he used profane language in private"; 30 percent, "if he saw a psychiatrist"; 21 percent, "if he wore blue jeans occasionally in the Oval Office"; 17 percent, "if he were divorced"; and 14 percent, "if he had a cocktail before dinner each night."

Finally, Edwards found that the public expects more of presidents today than it did in the past. In the fall 1979 Gallup poll, 73 percent of the respondents believed that the "public's expectations of the president are higher than [they were] in the past"; 77 percent believed the "problems presidents must solve are more difficult" today than in the past; 76 percent believed the "press is [now] more critical of the president"; and 75 percent believed "Congress is more difficult to deal with" than in the past. In summary, the findings Edwards cited suggest that the public sets very high standards for our president's behavior, both in public and in private (Edwards 1983: 189–191).

More recent data collected by the University of New Mexico's Institute for Public Policy suggests that the public continues to expect high standards of presidential performance (see Waterman, Jenkins-Smith, and Silva Forthcoming). Respondents were asked the following question: "Thinking about the kind of person you believe would be an excellent president, how important are the following four qualities?" The four qualities were: sound judgment in a crisis, experience in foreign affairs, high ethical standards, and an ability to work well with Congress. Respondents were asked to evaluate these qualities on a scale from 0 to 10, with 0 being "not at all important" and 10 being "extremely important." Polls of New Mexico residents were then conducted in January/February of 1996, at the beginning of Bill Clinton's reelection campaign, and in October/November 1996, at the end of the election year.

Part A of Table 1.1 presents the mean (or the average) responses for each of the four qualities, as related to the respondents' perceptions of excellent presidents. Regarding the quality of sound judgment in a crisis, in the January/February survey the average response on a 10-point scale was 9.08; this indicates that the possession of sound judgment was indeed considered to be a very important criterion for "excellent presidents." The results were similar for the October/November 1996 survey—the mean or average response was 9.20, again out of a possible 10 points. On the other hand, experience in foreign affairs was considered to be somewhat less important, with a mean of 7.49 in the first and 7.82 in the second survey. As for high ethical standards, the mean was 8.48 in the first poll and 8.58 in the second. Finally, the means for an ability to work well with Congress were 8.17 and 8.45, respectively. In summary, then, on all four leadership qualities, it is clear that respondents expected a great deal from the hypothetical "excellent president."

The same respondents were then asked to evaluate President Bill Clinton's performance based on the same four leadership qualities. As can be seen in Part B of Table 1.1, Clinton's rankings were not as high as the hypothetical excellent president. On sound judgment in a crisis, the mean response for Clinton was only 6.01 in the January/February survey and 6.58 in the October/November survey. Regarding experience in foreign affairs, Clinton ranked at just 5.35 in the first poll and 5.78 in the second. Considering the number of allegations regarding

TABLE 1.1
Four Measures of Presidential Job Characteristics

Part A: Means for the Four Qualities of Excellent Presidents

	January-February 1996	October-November 1996
Sound judgment in a crisis	9.08	9.20
Experience in foreign affairs	7.49	7.82
High ethical standards	8.48	8.58
An ability to work well with Congress	8.17	8.45

Part B: Means for Clinton's Evaluation on Basis of Four Qualities

	January-February	October-November
Sound judgment in a crisis	6.01	6.58
Experience in foreign affairs	5.35	5.78
High ethical standards	4.97	4.74
An ability to work well with Congress	4.47	5.85

Part C: Differences Between Qualities of Excellent Presidents and President Bill Clinton

	January-February	October-November
Sound judgment in a crisis	−3.07	−2.62
Experience in foreign affairs	−2.14	−2.04
High ethical standards	−3.51	−3.84
An ability to work well with Congress	−3.70	−2.60

Clinton's ethics—the Gennifer Flowers affair, allegations that he had avoided the draft, the Whitewater scandals, the Paula Jones sexual harassment lawsuit (questions about irregularities in campaign fund-raising and the allegation and subsequent admission that the president had an affair with White House intern Monica Lewinsky occurred after the two polls were conducted)—it is not surprising that the mean responses for Clinton on the issue of high ethical standards were only 4.97 and 4.74, respectively. Finally, with regard to an ability to work well with Congress, the mean for Clinton was just 4.47 in the poll at the beginning of the 1996 election year but 5.85 at the end. Clinton's improvement on this last measure was largely due to an increased level of cooperation between the president, a Democrat, and the Republican-controlled Congress in the summer of 1996, which led to the passage of minimum wage, health care reform, and welfare reform legislation.

In Part C of Table 1.1 we compare the results presented in Parts A and B. The mean responses for Bill Clinton's actual performance fell short of the evaluations of the hypothetical excellent president; the smallest difference was 2.14 points (for experience in foreign affairs), while the largest was 3.84 points (for high ethical standards). In both surveys the smallest differences related to experience in foreign affairs, while the largest differences were related to Clinton's ability to work well with Congress in the January/February survey and to the question of high ethical standards in the October/November survey. Clearly, then, the evidence suggests that this incumbent president, Bill Clinton, did not perform as well as the hypothetical excellent president.

The Impact of the Expectations Gap

What happens when presidents fail to satisfy the public's expectations? The evidence suggests that the public lays the blame directly at the front door of the White House itself. For example, a 1979 NBC-AP poll demonstrated that substantial numbers of respondents believed President Carter was at least partly to blame for continued high inflation, high energy prices, and gasoline shortages (Cronin 1980: 15), this despite the fact that he had inherited each of these problems from his predecessors, Richard Nixon and Gerald Ford. Carter was subsequently defeated in his bid for reelection.

Given the public's high expectations of presidential performance, presidential scholars have consistently argued that an **expectations gap** exists between what the public expects and what presidents can actually accomplish. They also contend that expectations are important, since expectations "shape evaluations, and evaluations, in turn, affect the capacity [of presidents] to get things done" (Stephen Wayne 1982: 185). Empirical research has demonstrated this point. In a classic article, James Stimson (1976) examined the approval ratings of several presidents and found a pattern of declining approval within each individual presidency over time. He attributed this phenomenon specifically to the expectations gap (Stimson 1976/77). Likewise, in an examination of the approval ratings of all elected first-term presidents from Eisenhower through Bush, Raichur and Waterman (1993) demonstrated "a near consistent pattern of declining presidential approval ratings over time," both within individual presidencies and across different presidencies. Finally, a more recent empirical study demonstrated that "the expectations gap both makes individuals less likely to approve of the president's job performance and less likely to vote for an incumbent. Furthermore . . . the wider each individual's perception of the gap is, the less likely they will be to approve of or vote for an incumbent president" (Waterman, Jenkins-Smith, and Silva Forthcoming).

Presidential scholars (for example, Rose 1997) have gone so far as to argue that since Lyndon Johnson's election to the presidency in 1964 there has been a near consistent pattern of presidential failure. Johnson, facing the mounting controversy engendered by the Vietnam War and a strong challenge from within his own party by Senator Eugene McCarthy, withdrew from his reelection contest in the spring of 1968. Three other presidents—Gerald Ford (1976), Jimmy Carter (1980), and George Bush (1992)—were defeated in their respective reelection campaigns. During this time period, three other presidents—Richard Nixon, Ronald Reagan, and Bill Clinton—were successfully reelected; but all three, facing a critical media and a belligerent Congress, endured scandals that dominated their second terms, with the possibility of impeachment and removal raised for Nixon and Clinton.

As a result of the **Watergate scandal**, Richard Nixon was forced to resign from office in disgrace, rather than face certain impeachment by the U.S. Congress. Ronald Reagan survived the **Iran-Contra scandal**, although his long-term historical reputation was damaged. As for Bill Clinton, the incumbent at the time this book was written, his presidency has been marked by a remarkable variety of allegations and scandals, the most damaging of which is the admission that he had sex with a White House intern only slightly older than his daughter (a scandal irreverently referred to by some as Zippergate). In an unprecedented action, in August of 1998, President Clinton testified before a federal grand jury that was, among other activities, considering his own possible criminal activity (perjury and obstruction of justice). Again, as with Nixon, articles of impeachment were adopted by the House Judiciary Committee.

Recent presidential history led one scholar, Theodore Lowi, to contend, "The probability of [presidential] failure is always tending toward 100 percent. . . . Given the exalted rhetoric and high expectations surrounding the presidency, a partial success [in policy terms] is defined as a failure"(1985: 11). Furthermore, there is no way to avoid this failure because expectations perpetuate themselves. In this regard Lowi wrote, "There are built-in barriers to presidents' delivering on their promises, and the unlikely occasion of one doing so would only engender another round of new policies, with new responsibilities and new demands for help" (ibid., 20). Consequently, as "presidential success advances arithmetically, public expectations advance geometrically." Lowi characterized this process as a "pathology because it escalates the rhetoric at home, ratcheting expectations upward notch by notch, and fuels adventurism abroad, in a world where the cost of failure can be annihilation." Lowi concluded, the "desperate search is no longer for the good life but for the most effective presentation of appearances."

Clearly, the expectations gap is a problem, perhaps the most serious problem facing the modern presidency. But is presidential failure always tending toward 100 percent? Is the presidency necessarily doomed to failure? Can presidents survive the expectations gap? One can credibly argue that reelection is one sign of presidential success. In that case, then, three recent presidents were successful in that they were elected to a second term.

Policy achievement is also evidence of presidential success. When we examine the policy agendas of our most recent presidents, we find that in 1981 Reagan succeeded in advancing a broad conservative economic program through Congress. Nixon was able to implement major changes in our nation's foreign policy, such as opening up contact with mainland China and détente with the Soviet Union. As for Clinton, he was able to work with a Republican-dominated Congress to balance the budget. Johnson, Carter, and Bush also had major policy successes. Lyndon Johnson managed to get the Civil Rights Act of 1964, the Voting Rights Act of 1965, and the Fair Housing Act of 1968 through an often hostile Congress. Medicare and other social programs were also created during his presidency. Carter played an integral role in the success of the Camp David Accords, which advanced the peace process in the Middle East. George Bush played a masterful role as commander-in-chief during the Persian Gulf War. Even Gerald Ford, who had little time to leave a mark on history, is credited with helping the nation heal its collective wounds following Nixon's resignation. Thus, while there is considerable evidence that public expectations are unrealistic, there also is evidence that all modern presidents have had some important successes. Extrapolating from Lowi's argument, because of the expectations gap these presidents did not receive the full credit they deserved for their policy accomplishments. Rather, policy accomplishment only encouraged the public to expect more from its presidents, thus further ratcheting up the standard for a successful president.

If policy success is not enough, how can presidents succeed? Is a successful presidency even possible? In this book we argue that presidents since Nixon have adopted a new strategy to deal with the public's excessive, contradictory, and unrealistic expectations. They have attempted to present the public with a compelling image of presidential leadership and success. We will argue that in relation to the modern presidency, "image is everything."

Images

America is a nation of images. It is the land of the free, the land of opportunity, a nation of rugged individualism, and a nation of heroic expansionism. Such images permeate our history books and our literature. Images are everywhere, yet each masks realities that are often difficult for us to reconcile. For example, America is the land of the free, yet our past is littered with counterexamples: from slavery to Jim Crow laws, and on to the internment of Japanese-Americans during World War II. America is the land of opportunity, yet it is also a nation of contrasts, of rich and poor, and a stubbornly persistent underclass that some say has few hopes or opportunities for a better future. America is the land of rugged individualism, yet mass marketing techniques encourage conformity, not individualism. The advertising moguls of Madison Avenue tell us how we should dress and what we should eat. Critics tell us what movies we should like, and pundits tell us what we should think about politics. Finally, our nation is one of heroic expansionism and of "manifest destiny." Yet this image masks, among other things, a genocidal policy toward Native Americans. Consequently, in America images are indeed everywhere.

The media, and particularly television, has only accentuated our desire for and consumption of new images. As Mary Stuckey (1991: 136–137) noted, "The images transmitted through television . . . take on an immediacy that print lacks. Reactions to events are speeded up, and public perceptions of issues and political actors can and do change practically overnight." Today our television and movie stars, our athletes, and even our politicians carefully craft images for public consumption. Furthermore, these images are disposable. They can, when necessary, be replaced with new and improved images. If one image no longer sells the answer is simple: Get a new one! If a rock or rap star's "bad-boy" image no longer sells records, then have him clean up his act, get married, and find God; in other words, present a new and more saleable image to the American public. What is remarkable is that the odds are favorable that the public will forget the old image and accept the new one with unquestioned enthusiasm. It is the image we respond to, not necessarily the reality behind it. Consequently, if a politician has an image for being tough, we will tend to overlook it if he or she occasionally seems to buckle under political pressure. We can reason that if somebody that tough was forced to compromise, then anyone could. The image conditions our reaction. It defines what we think and even how we evaluate success or failure. In this vein, Jimmy Carter's former Treasury Secretary, Michael Blumenthal, noted in describing Washington politics, "you can be successful if you appear to be successful . . . appearance is as important as reality" (quoted in Wilson 1989: 197). Images can provide politicians, especially presidents, with an appearance of success.

Not all images promote success, however. Images can be good or bad. Who defines an image and how it is defined are increasingly important political questions. In politics, candidates and incumbents spend considerable time and money cultivating a preferred image. The expertise provided by well-paid and seemingly omnipresent **political consultants** thus plays an ever more important role in both the electoral and governing processes. According to Robert Reich (1997: 261–262), Bill Clinton's first labor secretary, political consultants

> sell candidates exactly the way Madison Avenue sells corn flakes and soap. They do phone surveys, opinion polls, and in depth "focus groups" in a never-ending quest to discover what the public wants. They then use the techniques of advertising and marketing to convert the candidate into that product. At best, political consultants help men and women of principle win election by educating the public about what such candidates believe and why. At worst, political consultants fight ferociously against any spark of principle, fashioning a candidate whose only characteristic is his or her marketability.

Reich was troubled by the growth of political consultants, who he notes "until very recently" were not even "recognized as a legitimate profession' (ibid., 261). He concluded: "In an era when almost everything is bought and sold, when packaging and spin are often indistinguishable from reality, and when ulterior motives seem to lurk behind almost every friendly encounter, our democratic process needs help." Political consultants such as Dick Morris, President Clinton's own consultant, "are debasing . . . [democracy], and the people who hire them are playing with a fire that one day could consume all of us" (ibid., 262).

As Reich noted in his definition, the job of a political consultant is to sell his or her candidate to the American people. It is not to provide, as the political parties once did, a policy agenda to assist in the governance process after the election. In fact, issues may be dangerous. They may distract the public from the image the consultant is crafting for a particular candidate. Consultants not only craft images for their candidate, they also attempt to define or redefine the opposition candidate's image, usually in the most simple and unflattering terms possible. As 1988 Democratic presidential nominee Michael Dukakis learned, the worst thing that can happen to a politician is to have the opposition party define one's image. Dukakis was defined by the rival Bush campaign, and particularly by its political wizard-in-residence, Lee Atwater, as a "liberal," an image strongly at odds with Dukakis' record as governor of the state of Massachusetts. One of Dukakis' first acts as governor had been to slash social service programs in order to balance the state budget. This is hardly a liberal response. Yet the image of Dukakis crafted by the Bush campaign stuck. The *image* was far more important than any evidence which might have suggested a different reality.

Image creation is a serious business with critically important implications for the success of any politician. This is, of course, particularly true of the presidency. As Michael Riccards (1995: Vol. 1, xvii-xviii) wrote, "Although the successes of presidents are surely linked to concrete realities, such as economic stability or depression, the outcomes of military battles, and fair tax and tariff schedules, the office is more importantly linked to the realm of popular impressions and symbols in which facts and administrative feats are only building blocks that can support or undermine in partial ways these overall leadership impressions." Again it is underscored that images play an important role in the perceived success or failure of our presidents.

Since public expectations are most often aimed directly at the White House and its central occupant—although Kimball and Patterson (1997) also show that public expectations are directed at Congress—it is more important than ever for a president to control his or her image, and to present the right image to the American public. For example, if foreign threats abound, then the president must present an image of strength. Ronald Reagan successfully presented the image of a president who would stand up to communism, to terrorism, and to other foreign threats (even if in the end he actually did deal with the Communists regarding a new arms control treaty, and with terrorists when he traded arms for hostages with Iran). On the other hand, for all of his rhetorical bravado, Jimmy Carter was not able to convince the American public that he was really tough enough to combat terrorism in Iran or the Soviet invasion of Afghanistan.

Images depend greatly on the political concerns of the time. Carter adopted the wrong image when he gave his famous "malaise" speech. In contrast, Reagan provided an image of cheery optimism. He also demonstrated that America was willing to stand tough against all foreign enemies. He proved this by restoring a free government to the tiny nation of Grenada. Though Grenada is hardly one of the world's great military powers, this successful military venture proved to many Americans that our nation was still strong; this despite the concomitant deadly bombing of an American military barracks in Beirut. The image the White House wanted to sell prevailed, largely because it was an image the American people wanted to accept. Americans were tired of the image of military failure that had prevailed since the Vietnam War and were ready to celebrate a victory, even over one of such limited strategic significance as Grenada. Reagan thus presented the right image at the right time.

On the other hand, if the public cares more about the poor and dispossessed, then the president must present an image of compassion and caring. Bill Clinton has been particularly effective at creating the image of feeling the nation's collective pain. George Bush, on the other hand, could not master this image. Rather, he developed the image of a president out of touch with the needs of ordinary Americans. While one can argue that the recession that ultimately contributed to Bush's defeat in the 1992 presidential election was the result of a much overdue downturn in the business cycle, Bush's image as a wealthy man who, in his private boat, sped around the ocean fronting his exclusive Kennebunkport summer home surely contributed to his electoral defeat. In short, he had the wrong image at the wrong time. Having the previous image of standing tall, of standing up to Saddam Hussein, didn't matter much in the midst of a recession, even a relatively mild one by historical standards.

For successful presidents, then, the task is to craft an image appropriate to the circumstances of their time. The problem is that presidents are constrained in their ability to create images. As we will argue in Chapter 2, constraints come in the form of what we will call historical images of the presidency. A president cannot adopt the image of a "common man," as Gerald Ford and Jimmy Carter did, at a time when the public expects presidents to be great leaders. Presidents cannot adopt the image of a "master politician" in a time when the public resoundingly abhors politicians. Having the right presidential image means, in part, adapting to current historical trends.

A president's choice of image is also constrained by his or her own personality. As Mary Stuckey (1991: 73) has written, "There are two sides to the presidency: the public side, the appearances presidents construct, and the private side, the 'real' president. Most presidential images are a combination of these two sides, since the ideal that the president tries to convey is usually hampered or affected by the encroachment of the private side." Hence, it was difficult for George Bush, who had a patrician upbringing, to sell himself to the public as a man who understood the needs of average Americans. It would not have been an impossible task, however. Franklin Roosevelt also was also raised in wealth, but he consciously adopted an image that appealed to average Americans. When, for example, he invited the king and queen of England to the United States in 1939, he threw a hot dog roast in their honor at Hyde Park. He did not deny his patrician background—after all, he did hold the roast at Hyde Park—but by serving hot dogs, he sent the signal that he was, at heart, a quintessential American. Ordinary Americans could therefore directly relate to the patrician Roosevelt.

In addition, the effervescence and reassuring personality of Franklin Roosevelt, his image as a vital activist, was perfect for a nation in the midst of a depression. Eisenhower as "father figure" presented the perfect image for the less activist governmental era of the 1950s. John Kennedy's image of youthful idealism was a perfect one for the ferment of the 1960s. Following the failure of Vietnam, Reagan's image of toughness was ideal for the 1980s. On the other hand, despite his considerable accomplishments, Lyndon Johnson's dour image proved as electorally damaging as his Vietnam War policies. Gerald Ford's image as a likable "klutz" did little in 1976 to convince the public that he was qualified to be president. Likewise, Jimmy Carter's image of vacillation and ineffectiveness fueled his electoral defeat in 1980.

Presidents must therefore be careful in crafting their images. As we shall see in Chapter 2, Carter's decision in 1976 to create an image as a blue-jeans-wearing "common man" proved useful in getting him elected, but undermined his ability to govern once he arrived in Washington. He called himself just plain "Jimmy," sold the presidential yacht—the *Sequoia*—and halted the practice of playing "Hail to the Chief" at his public appearances. When the political opposition and the press began to portray just plain "Jimmy" as being a bit too common and therefore not quite up to the task of being president, Carter abandoned his blue jeans, brought back "Hail to the Chief," and attempted to exhibit himself in more appropriately presidential settings. Still, the image Carter had created in 1976 was never fully erased from the public's consciousness, and the perception that he was "too small for the job" stuck. Carter had lost the image war.

If presidents are to succeed, then, they must present an appropriate *image* of leadership to the American people, an image that meets the needs of the time when the president governs and also fits the personality of that president. Their ultimate goal is to convince the public that they are actually providing leadership, even if in reality they have only a limited ability to affect outcomes. Reality thus becomes secondary and image is everything.

Image Creation and Pseudo-Events

How exactly does one go about the task of creating a desired presidential image? According to Boorstin (1961: 11–12), images can be created through what he calls **pseudo-events.** As the name suggests, pseudo-events are events that are not genuine events. They are spectacles created for the sole purpose of creating an image. The basic characteristics of a pseudo-event are:

> (1) It is not spontaneous, but comes about because someone has planned, planted, or incited it . . . (2) It is planned primarily (but not exclusively) for the immediate purpose of being reported or reproduced. Therefore, its occurrence is arranged for the convenience of the reporting or reproducing media. Its success is measured by how widely it is reported. . . . The question, "Is it real?" is less important than, "Is it newsworthy?" . . . (3) Its relation to the underlying reality of the situation is ambiguous. Its interest arises largely from this very ambiguity . . . (4) Usually, it is intended to be a self-fulfilling prophecy.

An example of a pseudo-event would be when a president seeking the image of being tough on crime organizes an event at the White House Rose Garden. The president surrounds himself or herself with a phalanx of police officers, all formally uniformed, badges appropriately burnished for the cameras. The president then stares into the television cameras and intones something like, "Crime is my number one concern. We must stop the scourge of lawlessness that infests our streets." The police officers dutifully applaud as the president appears ever more resolute. The message is clear—this president is tough on crime. The reality, however, is not so clear. What will this president actually do? Nothing specific has been identified, discussed, analyzed, or accomplished. The president has merely said he is tough on crime. Yet the event, or pseudo-event, is dutifully reported by a media that is gleeful (even if cynical) about the great visual images the president has provided for their newscasts and front pages. The public witnesses a president who appears to be tough on crime. Yet not one criminal has been apprehended. Not one substantive step has been taken toward the apprehension of a criminal. Nor is one criminal likely to be apprehended as a result of this ceremony. Image creation was the only reason this pseudo-event took place. With crime perceived to be rampant in the streets, with polls indicating that people are particularly concerned about crime, it is imperative that the president *appear to be* tough on crime. Image is everything! If subsequent statistics indicate that this president has not done a particularly effective job in fighting crime, the president, his pollsters, his consultants, and his advisers all trust that the image they have carefully created will deflect any attack by the opposition party or the press.

Although pseudo-events have long been an important part of a president's political resources, in recent years presidents and their political consultants have become ever more skilled at utilizing them. Boorstin identified the Kennedy-Nixon debates of the 1960 presidential campaign as a particularly egregious example of a pseudo-event. According to Boorstin (1961: 41–42) the debates "were remarkably successful at reducing great national issues to trivial dimensions. . . . They were a clinical example of the pseudo-event, of how it is made, why it appeals, and of its consequences." As evidence Boorstin noted, "Public interest centered around the pseudo-event itself: the lighting, make-up, ground rules, whether notes should be allowed, etc. Far more interest was shown in the performance than in what was said." This pseudo-event then spawned additional pseudo-events:

> People who had seen the shows read about them more avidly, and listened eagerly for interpretations by news commentators. Representatives of both parties made "statements" on the probable effects of the debates. Numerous interviews and discussion programs were broadcast exploring their meaning. Opinion polls keep us informed on the nuances of our own and other people's reactions. . . . [But in the end, the] drama of the situation was mostly specious, or at least had an ambiguous relevance to the main (but forgotten) issue: which participant was better qualified for the pres-

idency. Of course, a man's ability, while standing under klieg lights, without notes, to answer in two and a half minutes a question kept secret until that moment, had only the most dubious relevance—if any at all—to his real qualifications to make deliberate presidential decisions on long-standing questions after being instructed by a corps of advisers.

In short, this pseudo-event created its own reality, one that Boorstin believed was irrelevant to the larger task of choosing a qualified president. But the pseudo-event successfully created images. The immediate manifestation of the vitality of Kennedy's performance was more enthusiastic crowds at subsequent campaign events, more favorable press coverage, and a new perception that Kennedy was indeed a man of presidential caliber. For Nixon, the resultant image was of a man politically vulnerable, even sinister. More has probably been written about Nixon's five o'clock shadow than about what he actually said in the debate. What ultimately proved to be important were the visual images broadcast into living rooms around America, and the perceptions of those reporters and pundits who watched the debates. One can argue that the 1960 presidential debates went far in creating the Kennedy mystique. But what did Kennedy's actual answers during the debate tell us about his qualifications to be president? A perusal of the scholarly literature about the debate will quickly indicate that few scholars have been interested in that particular question. Even in scholarly analysis, then, image can take precedence, and reality is somehow lost in the blur of the long-forgotten klieg lights.

And yet the irony is that, by comparison, the 1960 debates were far more substantive in content than any subsequent presidential debates. Now presidents practice jokes and one-liners with their political consultants in preparation for their debates, ever aware that these will be used as **sound bites** by the news media and in campaign advertisements throughout the remainder of the campaign. The debate's visual format and setting is as important, if not more so, than the content of the questions the candidates are asked or the answers they provide. More emphasis is placed on pre-debate strategy than on formulating or articulating a coherent vision of governance. Substantive stances often are considered dangerous because they may conflict with a candidate's desired image and because they may limit a president's ability to maneuver politically in the future.

As we shall discuss in the chapters to follow, policy substance often vastly conflicts with image creation. For example, in the case of the invasion of Grenada, the facts later indicated that the situation was not nearly as dire as President Reagan claimed in a televised speech to the nation, when he declared, "We got there just in time." Certainly, the military success in Grenada did not compare to the concomitant failure in Beirut, where more than 200 marines were murdered while they slept. From a substantive point of view, one could argue that the Reagan administration was negligent in placing the marines in harm's way. But the image that prevailed was not the one of military failure. Grenada worked as a pseudo-event because, as noted above, it presented an image that the American public was eager to embrace. No matter what the evidence might later indicate, Grenada exemplified the image Ronald Reagan and his advisers wanted to sell: America was standing tall.

Because images are often so at odds with reality, analysis of them is damaging. The public or the press aren't supposed to think too much about a good pseudo-event. Pseudo-events generally succeed on an impressionistic level. We see President Clinton sitting at a desk in front of the Grand Canyon signing an executive order setting aside federal land in Utah. We are not supposed to ask why the president is in Arizona if the order he is signing affects Utah. We are supposed to think, the president is sitting in front of the Grand Canyon. He must care about the environment. Since evidence and analysis can undermine pseudo-events, it is no wonder then why substance is devalued. In fact, since reality and images often conflict, political consultants often prefer to eschew substance entirely. In the end, if the public accepts the image, as it did following the Grenada invasion, then it is the image that matters, not the particular facts of the case. Again, image is everything.

Conclusions

In this book we will examine the impact of image making on the history and governance of the country. In the second and third chapters we will examine the historical and personal images presidents have adopted. In Chapters 4 and 5 we will turn our attention to one of the primary impacts of the "image-is-everything presidency": the elevation of style over substance. In Chapter 4 we examine how image has come to play a primary role in presidential elections while substance has come to take a much less important role. With elections more about image than issues, presidents are left in a much less appropriate position to govern once they are elected. In Chapter 5 we turn our attention to one of the primary tools of modern governance: presidential speechmaking. This chapter is particularly important since much of what happens in the modern presidency consists of such pseudo-events as presidential speeches (many of which are devoid of substance), spectacles, photo opportunities, and other staged events. How these events are staged and what presidents hope to gain from them will be the central thesis of the chapter. In Chapter 6 we will examine the nexus between the media and the presidency, since the media play a critical role in defining a president's image, and the media have over time developed an increasingly adversarial relationship with the presidency. Finally, in Chapter 7 we will synthesize the various lessons gleaned from this book and discuss the implications of the image-is-everything presidency for the future of the presidency.

2

··

Historical Images

I'm not a doctor, but I play one on TV.

—From a popular TV commercial

Abraham Lincoln splitting rails. Photo courtesy of Culver Pictures, Inc., reprinted with permission.

In this book we will be discussing two different types of presidential images. **Personal images** are the ones that individual presidents adopt in order to look tough on crime, strong on national defense, or compassionate toward the needs of the poor. **Historical images** are broader images that reoccur over time and generally reflect the prevailing attitudes of a particular era in American history. In this chapter we introduce and describe three historical images: the Common Man, the Master Politician, and the Washington Outsider. We will also discuss how these historical images shape and constrain an individual president's ability to adopt personal images.

For example, the **common man image** was popular during the nineteenth century and reflected the image of the president as an ordinary American. As the public came to expect its presidents to be more than ordinary individuals, the usefulness of the common man image declined. The **master politician image** was prevalent for much of the twentieth century. Presidents such as Theodore Roosevelt, Woodrow Wilson, and Franklin Roosevelt typified this new, more action-oriented presidency. In a more cynical age, however, the master politician has degenerated into an image of a politician who is perceived to be dishonest. The image that presidents presently cultivate is the **Washington outsider image**. While it has proven particularly useful in getting candidates elected to office, it has been less useful as a governing image, since presidents who come from the outside are less likely to understand or appreciate the nuance of Washington beltway politics.

In this chapter, we will also argue that image creation is not a static phenomenon, but rather one that has evolved over time. As one historical image is discredited or declines in usefulness, presidents turn to the formulation and cultivation of new images. Additionally, we will examine the relationship between the three historical presidential images and public expectations of the presidency. We will argue that the common man image was more suited to a time when public expectations were more modest. As public expectations increased, the master politician became a more useful historical image. Presidents governing under this image, however, also greatly increased public expectations. As for the Washington outsider image, presidents who adopt it may not have the necessary political skills to satisfy public expectations.

The President as Common Man

While the founding fathers created a representative form of government, they purposely limited the role of the public in it. The Constitution as originally written did not provide for the direct election of Senators. The president was to be selected by the Electoral College, not directly by the public. Justices and judges were to be appointed by the president and with the advice and consent of the Senate. Only the House of Representatives was popularly elected. Given the Founders' caution about democracy, it is not surprising that none of our first six presidents can be described as populists. Four were Virginia aristocrats and the two others were from the prestigious Adams family of Massachusetts. In sum, the idea of government by the people evolved only slowly over time.

By the 1820s, however, American politics had become more democratic. Over time suffrage had been extended to all white adult males and in most states the public, rather than the state legislatures, voted in presidential elections, though still for the Electoral College and not directly for the president. In addition, the electoral importance of the Western states, which included a more pioneer-oriented population, was increasing. The image of an Eastern, urbane, and educated (in other words, an aristocratic) candidate for president was thus becoming less useful electorally. Each of these factors helped to promote a new and enduring image of the president as a common man.

The seventh president of the United States, Andrew Jackson, became the personification of this new historical image, one that would influence American politics throughout the nineteenth century. Through direct appeals to the people, Jackson drew a connection with the common man that no other presidential candidate had ever done. In fact, he did so to such an extent that many members of the political aristocracy considered him a demagogic politician. Their fears seemed to have been realized on the night of Jackson's inauguration. In a demonstration of his support for the common man, Jackson invited ordinary Americans to celebrate his victory at the White House, which they, in their raucous enthusiasm for Jackson, damaged. As president, Jackson introduced the spoils system which removed many aristocratic individuals from various governmental posts and replaced them with party loyalists. His attack on the Bank of the United States can also be interpreted as a fight for the common man against a giant governmental institution.

Jackson was clearly successful in drawing a connection with the common man. In his eulogy of Jackson, Washington McCartney expressed the following sentiment (quoted in Ward 1955: 1):

> [Jackson] put himself at the head of the great movement of the age in which he lived. …Run the eye across the history of the world. You observe that there are certain cycles, or ages, or periods of time, which have their peculiar spirit, their ruling passion,

their great, characterizing, distinctive movements. He, who imbodies [sic] in its greatest fulness [sic], the spirit of such an age, and enters with most earnestness into its movements, received the admiration of his contemporaries. . . . And why? because [sic] they see in him their own image. . . . Because his countrymen saw their image and spirit in Andrew Jackson, they bestowed their honor and admiration upon him.

People saw "their image and spirit" in Jackson, yet in reality he was far from a common man. He had practiced law, been a member of the House of Representatives, a Senator (on two separate occasions), a Justice of the Tennessee Superior Court, and a general in both the War of 1812 and the First Seminole War (see Degregorio 1991: 110–111). Instead of portraying himself as a man of the people, Jackson could just as easily have identified himself as a man of considerable political experience. Jackson consciously adopted images that encouraged the public to accept him as one of them. His repeated electoral success—he was twice elected president and received the most popular and electoral votes in 1824 when the House of Representatives eventually chose John Quincy Adams as president—was a clear signal to other political elites of the power of the common man image. Despite their initial hesitancy, this signal was not lost on Jackson's political opponents.

In 1840 the Whig Party, which had deep philosophical differences with Jackson and his Democratic Party, consciously eschewed the issues and leaders who had previously led them to defeat, turning instead to issuing a more democratic appeal to the common man (Schlesinger 1945: 289). The Whigs rejected such able leaders as Daniel Webster and Henry Clay, instead choosing a "Westerner, a military hero, and a plain man of the people . . . William Henry Harrison." In reality, Harrison was no more a plain man of the people than Jackson had been. But when a Baltimore newspaper said that Harrison would be happy if he had "a pension, a barrel of hard cider, and a log cabin," an image far at odds with Harrison's actual background as a wealthy planter, the Whigs were ecstatic. Overnight, the Whigs became the party of hard cider and log cabins (Schlesinger 1945: 290–291). As Schlesinger wrote,

> Log cabins were everywhere—hung to watch chains and earrings, in parlor pictures and shop windows, mounted on wheels, decorated with coonskins and hauled in magnificent parades. Large ones were set up in the principal cities, surrounded by barrels of cider, with the latchstring dangling out in welcome for all comers. . . . Harrison himself, born a Virginia aristocrat, watched without protest his transmutation into a plain man of the people, while his spacious house in Ohio was reshaped into a humble log cabin. (ibid., 290–292)

Harrison even exchanged his "tall silk hat for a broad-brimmed rustic model . . . " (ibid., 292). The Whig's 1840 common man campaign was successful, even if Harrison's presidency was not; he died 30 days after assuming the presidential office. The lesson of 1840, however, was that image and reality did not have to converge. Even an aristocrat who claimed to be a common man could be elected to the presidency.

Of course, today when we think of log cabins, it is Abraham Lincoln who comes immediately to mind. Waldo Braden (1987: 267) has noted, "Lincoln presented himself [to Americans] as a common man." Likewise, Mary Stuckey (1991: 22) has written, "Lincoln used this image as a 'common man' combined with biblical clarity of expression to attain and keep popular support." Lincoln's common man image was in fact carefully crafted and sold to the American people. It was sold through the campaign biography, which was a common electoral technique at the time Lincoln was running for president in 1860. Biographies favorable to the candidate would be written, sold, and distributed throughout the nation with the active participation of the political parties. For example, John Locke Scripps' thirty-two page biography, which cost as little as two cents and sold approximately 200,000 copies (Schlesinger 1994, Vol. 1: 244–245) portrayed Lincoln as a common man. But the selling of Lincoln went far beyond mere campaign biographies. According to David Donald (1995: 244–245), Richard J. Ogelsby, a Lincoln supporter from Decatur, considered Lincoln's image as "Honest Abe" colorless. He believed that Lincoln needed a "more dynamic image." Ogelsby and John Hanks, a cousin of Lincoln's mother, "located a rail fence that Hanks and Lincoln had put up in 1830," and then took the rail to the Republican Convention. Lincoln was there announced as "Abraham Lincoln, The Rail Candidate." Donald continued, "The cheers that greeted Lincoln's remarks suggested that even his managers had underestimated his popularity. Now labeled 'the Rail Splitter' . . . he acquired an image with enormous popular appeal: he could be packaged not merely as a powerful advocate of the free-soil ideology or as a folksy unpretentious, storytelling campaigner, but also as the embodiment of the self-made man . . ."

On the stump, Republicans "emphasized Lincoln's humble origins, portraying the candidate as a self-made man and hence a symbol of democracy." An "industry in Lincoln rails soon developed . . ." In addition, "[b]anners and transparencies pictured Lincoln in rude western garb with an axe; split rails or a log cabin were often also visible." Furthermore, "Republicans routinely referred to their candidate as Honest Abe, Honest Old Abe, or just Old Abe in order to enhance his image as a common man" (Schlesinger 1994: Vol 1, 247).

Again, as in the cases of Jackson and Harrison, there is some question about the veracity of these images. David Donald (1995: 245) has written, "It mattered very little that this myth—like most myths—was only partially true: Lincoln, in fact, had little love for his pioneer origins; he disliked physical labor and left it as soon as he could; he owed his early advancement as much to the efforts of interested friends . . . as to his own exertions. Rather than a simple backwoodsman, he was a prominent and successful attorney representing the most powerful interests in emerging corporate America." It is clear that Lincoln was not comfortable with his own frontier background. As Stephen Oates (1984: 36) noted, "One thing [Lincoln] felt 'most deeply' was his log-cabin origins. The truth is that he felt embarrassed about his frontier past and never liked to talk about it." Lincoln even loathed the name Abe—as in "Honest Abe" and "Old Abe"—to such an extent that his wife Mary called him "Mr. Lincoln" or "Father" (Oates 1984: 51). Perhaps the only image that Lincoln was truly proud of was his reputation for impeccable honesty. As Oates (52) commented, ". . . Lincoln was as honest in real life as in the legend." But other than this image for honesty, Lincoln had spent his entire life prior to his first presidential run in 1860 distancing himself from these common man images.

As these examples demonstrate, during the nineteenth century, many candidates and their supporters crafted images that appealed to the common man. This common man image was still useful in the early twentieth century. In the 1920s Calvin Coolidge consciously developed and employed this image to great effect. As Michael Riccards (1995: Vol. 2, 102–103) has noted,

> [Coolidge] said little, calculated carefully, and established overnight a homey New England image. He took the oath of office from his father in a Vermont farmhouse lit by kerosene lamps. Once in Washington, he tried to sit in front of the White House in a rocking chair, just as he would sit on the porch of an old Yankee homestead.

Unlike many other common man presidents, "Coolidge successfully created his homey image in part because he genuinely lived it" (Riccards 1995: 103). The image clearly served his political purposes, however. Following the political and financial scandals of the Harding administration, Coolidge "was instrumental in restoring public confidence in the American political system" (McCoy 1988: ix). If Harding came to be perceived as corrupt, Coolidge came to embody honesty. Like Lincoln, he could be trusted because he exhibited the best qualities of the American people themselves.

Harry Truman was the next common man president—Alonzo Hamby (1995) even titled his book about Truman *Man of the People*. By the time Truman was inaugurated, however, public expectations of the presidency had changed and the usefulness of the historical common man image began to decline. Prior to Franklin Roosevelt's presidency, and the establishment of the modern presidency, many presidents had successfully cultivated the common man image. While elites may have questioned whether Andrew Jackson was qualified to be president (mostly they seemed to be concerned about his crude manner) and while even Lincoln's cabinet questioned whether the newly elected president was capable of leading the nation during the Civil War, most nineteeth-century presidents were not unduly burdened by the common man image once they entered the White House. For Truman, however, the image proved highly detrimental. Because he followed Franklin Roosevelt, many people simply did not believe that Truman was qualified to be president.

Why did the common man image that had served presidents up through Calvin Coolidge so well suddenly serve Truman so poorly? The answer appears to be that public expectations of the presidency had changed radically following the election of Franklin Roosevelt. *The public now expected the president to lead the nation.* Furthermore, it was unclear to many how anyone could fill Roosevelt's prodigious shoes. As David McCullough (1992: 349) wrote, "To many it was not just that the greatest of men had fallen, but that the least of men—or at any rate the least likely of men—had assumed his place." Everywhere the reaction was the same: "If Harry Truman can be President, so could my next-door neighbor" (ibid.).

In twelve-plus years Franklin Roosevelt had transformed the people's expectations of the presidency. It was now an office that no mere mortal—or common man—could be expected to inhabit. An extraordinary man was now required for governing; and the consensus was that Harry Truman was not an extraordinary man. Clearly, the image of a common man was more amenable to the more leisurely governing style of the nineteenth and early twentieth centuries.

With extraordinary skill, Truman was able to mitigate at least some of these public concerns about his capabilities. He did this by assuming leadership on the world stage. His many accomplishments (the Truman Doctrine, the Marshall Plan, the development of the modern Defense Department, U.S. membership in the United Nations and NATO) all contributed to many people's new perception of him as indeed a capable leader. Still, even with all of his international accomplishments, the popular perception of Harry Truman as a common man, not quite up to the job of being president, was never fully eradicated. Throughout his presidency, the public would continue to have nagging doubts about Truman's capabilities.

Truman's experience should have provided a clear signal to his successors that public expectations of the presidency had changed, and with it the value of the common man image. Of the post-FDR presidents, Dwight Eisenhower was clearly the most successful at cultivating a common man image. But Eisenhower was the exception among other twentieth-century presidents. He invoked two images concomitantly: his image as a "humble man of the people," exemplified by his 1952 "I like Ike" campaign for the presidency, and his heroic image, created by his extraordinary wartime performances (Stuckey 1991: 53). Mary Stuckey has argued that these two images are "contradictory." Yet a case can be made that they actually complement one another. Eisenhower was capable of portraying himself as a humble, ordinary man *because* he had done extraordinary and heroic things. His heroic image therefore mitigated any concerns that his common man image may have raised. In other words, no one could intimate that Eisenhower was not a big enough man to be president.

The next common-man president, Gerald Ford, did not have Eisenhower's military background or heroic reputation. Ford's initial return to the common man image made perfect political sense. Like Coolidge following the scandals of the Harding presidency, Ford adopted the common man image as a means of presenting a stark contrast to his predecessor, Richard Nixon. Nixon's personal image had devolved into that of a neurotic, solitary man at a desk, out of touch with reality. In contrast, Ford was perceived as an honest, regular guy. When Ford assumed the presidency, the press reported "he dances, he prays, he walks onto his front lawn in his bathrobe to get his morning paper. He makes his own breakfast, he swims, he holds meetings, he sleeps in the same bed as his wife" (quoted in DiClerico 1993: 116). At first the common man image bolstered Ford's credibility. But over time, as had happened with Truman, Ford's image as a regular guy became a political liability. As Michael Riccards (1995: Vol. 2, 359–360) wrote,

> The president's image became one of a man of limited intellectual gifts, a bumbler, and a boob who stumbled, literally, over his own feet. He became the subject of humor, and worst of all ridicule for these alleged faults, when he probably was the most physically fit and coordinated president in recent times. But image in politics pushes against reality, and Ford's achievements were being overwhelmed by real difficulties and some false barbs.

As with Truman, the problem was that the image of a common man intimated that Ford was not an exceptional enough man to be an effective president. Being a regular guy was O.K. in the short term, but as a long-term governing strategy it held significant liabilities. As Mary Stuckey (1991: 96) noted,

> In taking a "common man" approach, Ford . . . hurt his stature as president. Even in anti-imperial days, Americans appreciate and expect a certain level of elegance from presidents. They must appear to be of the mass and, at the same time, above it. Ford concentrated at being "one of us" to the point where we lost respect for him as "one of them." He earned affection at the price of respect.

Since he could not fall back on another image, as Eisenhower had done, Ford's common man image degenerated into a cruel caricature. Over time the press came to portray him as a likable klutz. "This image began after he fell from an airplane ramp in Salzburg, Austria, and it became an ongoing image problem. . . . In part, this may have been related to a suspicion among the press that Ford was not up to the job" (Stuckey 1991: 97).

Like Truman, Ford attempted to deal with his image problem by moving to the center of the world stage. As Riccards (1995: Vol. 2, 351) commented, "To deal with some long-standing commitments and to bolster his image as president, Ford undertook in late 1974 a series of trips abroad." But while Truman governed at a time of major international crisis, Ford's trips were not nearly as consequential. As a result, his strategy did not work. "Ford failed to understand that his problem was one of image and communication, not necessarily of substance" (Stuckey 1991: 97). Simply stated, his common man image was perceived by the public as contrary to that of a strong president. Stuckey has noted, "Ford's biggest problem was that he tried to combine two contradictory images: those of the 'guy next door' and 'Mr. President'" (ibid., 98). He was seen as lacking the toughness, even ruthlessness, to be president. Stuckey continued, "We may like the boy next door . . . , [but] we do not want him to be president" (ibid., 102).

Ironically, the man who defeated Ford for the presidency in 1976, Jimmy Carter, suffered much the same fate as his predecessor. Like Ford, Carter actively cultivated an image of himself as a trustworthy, common man. He wore blue jeans, called himself just plain "Jimmy," rather than James, told the American people he would never lie to them, and reminded voters that he was a simple peanut farmer. The common man campaign of 1976 helped Carter win the election, but this same image eventually undercut his credibility as president.

Like Ford, Carter made the mistake of not appearing to be presidential. He proudly announced that "we decided to forgo the 'Ruffles and Flourishes' and 'Hail to the Chief'" (Stuckey 1991: 103). He meant to show the nation that he was not a politician, and certainly not an imperial president. But when Carter suffered a series of legislative setbacks early in his term, and when he blundered by threatening to cancel a number of water projects near and dear to the hearts of important members of Congress, the verdict was quick and brutal: Carter lacked the necessary experience to be president. As president Carter also had the misfortune to be faced with a variety of difficult and persistent problems, including high inflation, high unemployment, and high interest rates. He watched helplessly as the economy twice fell into recession, as the Soviets moved troops into Afghanistan, and as Americans were taken hostage in Iran. Each of these events contributed to a new image of Carter as a man who lacked experience and toughness. When in the spring of 1980 Carter attempted a daring rescue mission to free the hostages, a mission that ended in abject failure, it "did little to improve the beleaguered president's image" (Rose 1997: 71). Ultimately his personal image became one of incompetence and failure. In short, Carter, like Ford, was never able to overcome the perception that he was not big enough for the job. Sadly, both Ford and Carter "left office tainted with the image of incompetence, having lost their bids for reelection. Yet both men were successful to the extent of being considered honest men who did their best for a troubled nation" (Stuckey 1991: 92). Being an honest failure, however, was not the image their successors desired.

The President as a Master Politician

Barbara Hinckley (1990: 7) described our first president, George Washington, as a "practical man, highly successful, yet modest and religious" who accepted "his country's honors; all the while pointing out how much" he disliked "power" and instead how he desired only "a humble private life." As Barry Schwartz (1987) has argued, Washington played an active role in creating his own image as a man who was undesirous of power. The values and images Washington symbolized, such as duty, selflessness, and patriotism, became the values with which his successors wanted to be associated. Perhaps as importantly, they also became values (and symbols) that the public came to expect from their presidents throughout the nineteenth century. Hence, in the process of creating his own image, Washington (whether by design or not) established important standards for future presidents.

Throughout the nineteenth century, following Washington's lead, it became unseemly for a prospective presidential candidate to appear to be motivated by political ambition. Presidential candidates were expected to publicly disavow any interest in the presidency, thus making their nomination appear to be bestowed because of their exemplary qualities but against their wishes. Once nominated, they were not expected to campaign for office. That task was left to a variety of party surrogates. Even after they were elected, our early presidents often spoke wistfully of the days ahead when the burdens of office would be removed and they would be free to return to private life.

Of course, in reality many of these presidents were indeed very ambitious men. For example, James Monroe worked diligently and sometimes even ruthlessly to secure the position of Secretary of State—at the time a stepping stone to the presidency—during James Madison's presidency. Likewise, in 1796 Thomas Jefferson publicly disavowed any interest in running for president. His private correspondence, however, provide evidence of political ambition (Ellis 1997). But while presidents could write about their personal ambitions in private, any public utterance along these lines would have represented political suicide.

This political norm helps explain why few politically prominent politicians were elected to the presidency during the nineteenth century. Furthermore, most of those with vast political experience proved to be failures. Martin Van Buren's reputation as a politician certainly proved detrimental during his single term in office. Presidents rarely actively used even their clearly articulated constitutional authority. Reflecting this point, nineteenth-century presidents were regularly referred to as the Chief Magistrate, a term that does not suggest presidential power. In contrast, in the twentieth century, presidents have been regularly referred to as the Chief Executive or Commander-in-Chief. Those nineteenth-century presidents who actively employed presidential power were regularly characterized by their opponents as kings, tyrants, and dictators. Andrew Jackson was derisively referred to as a king. Even his opposition party's name, the "Whig" party, was chosen because in England the Whig Party had fervently rejected the use of broad executive power. James K. Polk's extraordinary use of presidential power opened him up to savage congressional attacks. One of Polk's most vehement critics was a one-term congressman from Illinois named Abraham Lincoln. Ironically, during the Civil War Lincoln would be accused of being both a dictator and a tyrant. Clearly, then, the nineteenth-century American public felt more comfortable with individuals who, whatever their past electoral or governmental experience might be, appeared, at least in public, to be unambitious, even casual about their interest in the presidency. Simply stated, the public expectations of the time did not favor the broad use of executive authority. The president was seen as the Chief Magistrate, an executor and arbiter, not necessarily as a leader of the nation.

By the dawn of the twentieth century, however, America was undergoing a radical transformation. The nation was well on the road to industrialization, its citizens were deserting farms for the cities (where demands for governmental action were much more common), and America was taking its first steps onto the world stage. These social changes promoted political changes, including a new and expanded role for the president of the United States.

Theodore Roosevelt appears to have instinctively realized that times had changed. He certainly took full advantage of his constitutional authority, providing the presidency with a new and more expansive interpretation of presidential power. According to Roosevelt, rather than the constitution providing a list of presidential powers and duties that greatly constrained the president's ability to act, "the executive power was limited only by specific restrictions and prohibitions appearing in the Constitution or imposed by the Congress under its Constitutional powers." In other words, Roosevelt believed the president "was a steward of the people bound actively and affirmatively to do all he could for the people . . ." (Roosevelt 1985 edition: 371–372). This innovative—some might even refer to it as a dangerous—constitutional theory would play an important role in freeing presidents from the narrowly drawn constraints enumerated by Article II of the Constitution. It would be an important element in the development of both an activist presidency and of a new historical presidential image—the Master Politician image.

Though Roosevelt came to the White House with an image as a hero of the Spanish-American War, he could hardly be considered a common man. He was Harvard-educated and had a wealthy and socially prominent upbringing. Yet, if he couldn't be a common man, then he could use newly evolving media technologies to speak directly to the common man. Roosevelt's primary tool for such communication was the print media. He used newspapers in a way no other president ever had. He actively cultivated press coverage by inviting reporters into the Oval Office for personal conversations. He then provided them with information, which more often than not was beneficial to his policies and his preferred presidential image (Miller 1992: 326–327).

Roosevelt also became the most photographed president up to that time, being photographed performing all sorts of activities from hiking and equestrian sports, to operating a crane at the construction site for the Panama Canal. But he would not allow himself to be photographed playing tennis, because it was considered to be an effete sport, the exact opposite of the image of a virile man of action that Roosevelt actively wanted to cultivate (from the PBS documentary, *TR*). Through these and other mechanisms (for example, personal tours of the nation and the newly evolving cinema, which presented Roosevelt directly to millions of Americans), Teddy Roosevelt personalized the presidency in a way no nineteenth-century president ever had or could have, given the limited media technologies of that century.

Roosevelt was also more willing to use executive power than any president since Abraham Lincoln. He prodded Congress to adopt the Pure Food and Drug Act and legislation providing the government with greater authority in antitrust cases. He even articulated a far-reaching progressive agenda, which he called the "Square Deal." Still, the political norms of the time limited his ability to more aggressively pursue his political vision in domestic affairs. Roosevelt was therefore much more active in foreign affairs, where his constitutional authority was less constrained. He played a vital, perhaps even an unseemly role, in securing the site for the construction of the Panama Canal (see McCullough 1977). He developed the Roosevelt Corollary to the Monroe Doctrine to halt European aggression in South and Central America. He also played a critical role in settling the Russo-Japanese War, for which he was awarded the Nobel Peace Prize.

Yet, despite his many political accomplishments, Michael Riccards (1995, Vol. 2, 1) has written, ". . . Roosevelt's astonishing political career was formed not by a string of lasting achievements, but by a chimera of fleeting, but powerfully imposed images" It is clear that image creation played a major role in Roosevelt's presidency and that all these images revolved around action. It is also clear that at times, these images did not match reality. For example, Roosevelt cultivated a tough-talking public image by citing the African proverb, "Walk softly and carry a big stick." But as Nathan Miller (1992: 385) commented, the reality was somewhat different; "the Stick was more of a useful image than a reality." In the Santa Domingo crisis, for example, Roosevelt was clearly reluctant to use the big stick of American military power (see Brand 1998: 524–526).

Image also plays a major role in our perceptions of Roosevelt the trustbuster. While "Roosevelt was not in general an advocate of breaking up corporations, his exercise of presidential power" in such select cases as those involving Standard Oil, the New Haven Railroad, DuPont, and the American Tobacco Company "led to a popular, and then historical, image that he was a great 'trustbuster'" (Riccards 1995: Vol. 2, 8). In reality, however, Roosevelt's successor, William Howard Taft, was actually far more active and more successful as a trustbuster than Roosevelt. Yet, it is Teddy Roosevelt, not Taft, that history remembers. As Riccards (1995: Vol. 2, 33) commented, "It is odd that Roosevelt, who seemed so confident in office, so sure of his objectives, so skillful in his use of power, actually accomplished less in terms of legislative achievements than Taft, who was tagged as being inept and weak. In history, as in life, appearance is often a greater reality than experience itself."

But there was substance behind Roosevelt's images, as well. For example, while he toured the country in 1903 to include "some public hunting trips designed to further" his "image as a great outdoorsman" (Riccards 1995: Vol. 2, 16), he also set aside large quantities of land to be safe from developers. But Roosevelt's most important accomplishment was stylistic. He demonstrated that the president could occupy and dominate the center stage of American politics; likewise, he could be an active player on the world stage. In providing these lessons, Theodore Roosevelt laid the groundwork for the creation of the modern presidency, a new activist presidential model, and the image of the president as a master politician.

These accomplishments were not lost on one of Teddy Roosevelt's successors. In his classic 1885 book, *Congressional Government*, Woodrow Wilson advocated the establishment in the United States of a parliamentary-style governmental system to deal with the inherent weakness of the presidency and the decentralized anarchy caused by the congressional committee system. After Roosevelt's presidency, however, Wilson expressed a decidedly different opinion. In his 1908 book, *Constitutional Government in the United States*, Wilson argued, "there can be no mistaking the fact that we have grown more and more inclined from generation to generation to look to the President as the unifying force in our complex system, the leader both of his party and of the nation" (Wilson 1981 edition: 60).

As an academic, Wilson began to argue the possibilities of presidential leadership. As president he followed Roosevelt to the center of the domestic and world political stages. He was the first president since John Adams to deliver the State of the Union address in person before Congress. He played a much more active role as a legislative president than had Teddy Roosevelt, using the party system to encourage Congress to pass a sweeping series of progressive reforms, ironically many of them championed by Teddy Roosevelt in his 1912 Progressive/Bull Moose campaign for the presidency. In foreign affairs, Wilson sent troops to Mexico, to Russia, and then to Europe to fight in the Great War (World War I). He then personally traveled to Versailles to negotiate the peace treaty ending the war, actively urged other world leaders to establish the League of Nations, and traveled across the United States in an ultimately failed attempt to sell the treaty to the American people. Wilson's activism, like Roosevelt's, redefined the parameters of presidential power, as well as advanced a new historical image of an activist, master politician.

Largely as a result of Wilson's activism, however, the 1920s ushered in a decade of presidential passivity. In sharp contrast to the activist presidential model, the images that emerged during the 1920s were of Warren G. Harding napping with some of the great men of history (for example, Thomas Edison and Henry Ford) and Calvin Coolidge sleeping twelve hours a day! Such images of passivity reaffirmed that these presidents would not be active governing presidents. The usefulness of such images proved to be transitory, however. When the nation's economy collapsed in 1929, the public again looked to Washington and to the president for action. The public was now ready for the development of a new historical image of the presidency.

Franklin Delano Roosevelt (FDR) established not only the modern presidency, but also developed the image of the president as a master politician. Roosevelt's activism, and his mastery of politics, was apparent from his famous first 100 days, when Roosevelt declared a national bank holiday, reduced government spending, moved to legalize liquor sales, took the country off the gold standard, provided assistance for farmers and home owners, created the Tennessee Valley Authority, and provided support for organized labor (Leuchtenburg 1963: Chapter 3). In subsequent years, FDR's New Deal produced a number of other substantive accomplishments, including the enactment of Social Security for the aged, child labor laws, the Wagner Act to protect organized labor, and the Securities and Exchange Act to regulate unsavory trading practices on Wall Street. It is fair to say that FDR's New Deal policies directly impacted virtually every avenue of American life.

During World War II he was perhaps even more active. From "Dr. New Deal" Franklin Roosevelt became "Dr. Win the War." He prodded a reluctant Congress to create the first peacetime draft in American history, greatly expanded the size and capabilities of the army and navy, worked to preserve Great Britain and the Soviet Union through the innovative Lend-Lease program, and played a critical role in defining the parameters of the postwar world, including the creation of the United Nations. Domestically, he guided the nation's conversion from a peacetime to wartime economy, oversaw a massive increase in the production of military equipment, placed restrictions on the purchase of various products, and imposed a wage and price freeze. While only minimal progress was made in some areas, particularly civil rights, Franklin Roosevelt's programs transformed the nation.

In the process, he also transformed the presidency and, perhaps more importantly, public perceptions of it. The activist presidency that he created became the model for his successors. Scholars were quick to advocate this new presidential leadership model. In one of the most influential books written about the presidency, Richard Neustadt (1980 edition: 28) provided a veritable manual for the use of presidential power. He argued that the "power to persuade is the power to bargain." His description of the bargaining president was largely based on his own perceptions of the leadership styles of Franklin Roosevelt and his successor, Harry Truman. Roosevelt, in particular, had been the quintessential bargaining president, a master political manipulator. Now, his methods were being described by scholars as revealed wisdom. Among those who read Neustadt's book was John Kennedy, and all presidents through Bill Clinton have listened attentively to Neustadt's advice.

Other scholars promoted FDR's activist presidential model. Historian James MacGregor Burns (1965: 330) was representative of this school of thought when he wrote, the "stronger we make the Presidency, the more we strengthen democratic procedures." Clinton Rossiter (1960: 15–16) likewise spoke of the "veneration, if not exactly reverence, for the authority and dignity of the Presidency." And Herman Finer (1960: 119) commented, "the presidential office is no trifle, light as air, no bauble; it belongs rightfully to the offspring of a titan and Minerva husbanded by Mars." Franklin Roosevelt raised scholarly perceptions of the presidency to truly mythic proportions, which would make it an easy target once reality had a chance to settle in.

Roosevelt also altered the public's expectations of the presidency itself. In his 1944 State of the Union address, FDR promised the American people an "Economic Bill of Rights." He promised Americans that the U.S. government would assume responsibility for the "economic security and prosperity of all" (Sundquist 1981: 62). This promise led to later congressional passage of the Employment Act of 1946, which officially "committed the government to a continuous policy of economic activism" (ibid., 63). The public now had a reason to expect its presidents to provide them with a sound economy. As Edward Tufte (1978) would later empirically demonstrate, presidents who did not were not likely to be reelected.

On many other issues, the public likewise began to look to the White House for solutions. Those presidents who were capable of satisfying the public's escalating expectations were generally rewarded with reelection, while those who could not generally suffered electoral defeat. Most presidents after Franklin Roosevelt found that they had to be activists in order to satisfy the public's expanding demands; Eisenhower was a rare exception, though Fred Greenstein (1982) does make a convincing case that Eisenhower was more activist than most people thought at the time, governing through a "hidden hand" approach. Unfortunately, presidential activism encouraged the public to expect even more from the White House, more perhaps than presidents could reasonably be expected to deliver. FDR's successors found that their promises promoted an even further expansion of public expectations. Candidates for office made more generous promises in order to get elected, which encouraged the public to expect more action from its presidents, which in turn encouraged presidents to promise more action, which further encouraged the public to expect more from their presidents. This cycle of rising expectations created the conditions for inevitable failure (see Lowi 1985). One of the key problems with the activist presidential model and the master politician image, then, is that presidents eventually were hard-pressed to assuage the public's ever increasing demands for action.

This was a long-term problem, however. In the short term the activist approach paid extraordinary political dividends. Franklin Roosevelt was elected to the presidency an unprecedented four times, is ranked by most historians as one of the nation's best presidents, and left behind legacies in domestic and foreign affairs that dwarf the accomplishments of all other presidents. For Roosevelt, then, his image as a master politician certainly succeeded. As James MacGregor Burns (1984: ix) has written, "Roosevelt was one of the master politicians of his time.... His political artistry grew out of long experience with the stuff of American politics." Speaking of his governing style, Doris Kearns Goodwin (1994: 137) has noted, "Whereas critics decried his clever tricks as evidence of manipulation and deception, admirers considered such sleight of hand the mark of a master politician."

Of course, the ultimate irony of Franklin Roosevelt's presidency is that in contrast to his image for activism, he was actually unable to walk. It always comes as a surprise to students of our generation to learn that most Americans in the 1930s and 1940s did not know that FDR was confined to a wheelchair. The public knew that he had had polio in the 1920s and they were aware that he wore braces and *sometimes* used a wheelchair, but most Americans did not know the full nature of Roosevelt's health problems. It is also clear that Roosevelt purposely misled the public on this front. In public he was often photographed while standing; only a few photographs showing FDR sitting in a wheelchair exist, and they are all private photographs. Roosevelt even created a method that made it appear as if he were walking. While he held a cane in one hand, someone else (often his son) would grip his other hand, then Roosevelt would swing one leg around. Roosevelt would then push off with the cane to move the other leg, thus providing the appearance that he had actually walked (see Gallagher 1985; PBS documentary on FDR).

Roosevelt feared that if people thought he couldn't walk, they would not accept his image as an activist president. Consequently, while Roosevelt could not walk, he traveled more than any previous president in U.S. history. He traveled widely across the United States. He traveled aboard a destroyer in the U-boat-infested waters of the Atlantic Ocean to meet with British Prime Minister Winston Churchill. He also flew more than any president, even becoming the first presidential candidate to fly to his own political convention to accept his nomination in person. Roosevelt appeared vital in other ways, as well. On the radio his voice radiated vitality. Photographs portrayed his beaming smile, which transmitted his infectious confidence to the nation. To all appearances, then, Franklin Roosevelt was indeed a man of action. These are the personal images Roosevelt cultivated to promote his historical image as an activist president and as a master politician.

FDR's grand deception regarding his inability to walk unfortunately also extended to other areas of his presidency. He misled the American public about the state of his health when he ran for president in 1944. No mention was made of his congestive heart failure or his other serious physical problems. Roosevelt was also willing to mislead the public policywise. For instance, he was not adverse to signaling his support for the rights of African Americans in private, then doing nothing in public so as not to offend southern legislators who controlled most of the important congressional committees. Clearly, deception was an important part of FDR's leadership style.

This approach is best exemplified by a comment Roosevelt made on May 15, 1942. With regard to his foreign policy, FDR noted, "You know I am a juggler, and I never let my right hand know what my left hand does. . . . I may have one policy for Europe and one diametrically opposed for North and South America. I may be entirely inconsistent, and further I am perfectly willing to mislead and tell untruths, if it will help win the war" (quoted in Kimball 1991: 7). This statement, and other evidence of his willingness to deceive, reveal a Machiavellian tendency in the master politician image. Though aware of this propensity, most of FDR's biographers overlooked his inconsistencies and even his tendency to prevaricate, treating it instead as one price of great leadership. With FDR, then, a dark side of the master politician image emerged, one that eventually proved to be highly damaging to that image's long-term credibility with the American public.

Lyndon Johnson, one of Roosevelt's protégés, certainly had many of the necessary skills to be a great president. Like FDR, his list of legislative accomplishments is impressive: It includes the enactment of the Civil Rights Act of 1964, the Voting Rights Act of 1965, the Fair Housing Act of 1968, and the creation of the Medicare and Medicaid programs and Head Start. His legislative success was largely due to his bargaining skills. Johnson was extraordinarily effective in one-on-one situations. But by the 1960s television was forcing politics into the open. Rather than debating an issue collegially in private, policy makers were expressing their differences directly to the public. Individuals who were effective on television, such as Johnson's predecessor John F. Kennedy, were therefore at a distinct advantage. While FDR had been a master of the use of radio, Lyndon Johnson proved to be the very antithesis of the telegenic president. No matter how much Johnson tried to improve his delivery or appearance, he never appeared sincere on television. The public simply could not trust him. In short, television made Johnson look like a crass politician. As Mary Stuckey (1991: 75) has written, while "Kennedy had been noted for his 'style': Johnson's very skill was demeaning—he was a politician."

With the political environment and public perceptions changing so radically, the days of the master politician image were numbered. The credibility problems raised by Johnson's escalation of the war in Vietnam (after he seemed to have promised the electorate in the 1964 campaign that American "boys" would not fight in that war), the growing social unrest that was running rampant through the nation's major cities (evidenced by the riots in Watts, Detroit, and other cities), and the nature of many of Johnson's Great Society programs raised fundamental questions about Johnson's personal veracity and the proper role of the federal government. The presidency of Richard Nixon likewise seemed to divide the nation, even before the Watergate scandal forced Nixon from office. The Johnson and Nixon presidencies raised fundamental questions about the utility of the master politician image. At a time when anti-big government rhetoric was already prevalent and the word *politician* was taking on a decidedly more negative connotation, presidents and presidential candidates began to search for a new and more politically attractive historical image. They would find it in a resounding denunciation of traditional politicians, including master politicians, and anything having to do with Washington and the federal government.

The Washington Outsider Image

Andrew Jackson was the first president to adopt an image as an outsider (Milkis and Nelson 1994: 123). But following Richard Nixon's presidency, the Washington outsider image became the prevalent image in American politics. During the era of the master politician, people in Washington actively cultivated an image as a Washington insider. Politicians wanted their constituents to know that they were where the action was. They were in the halls of power. In other words, they were leaders.

By the 1970s, however, following the failure of the Johnson and Nixon presidencies, politicians began distancing themselves from Washington. Politicians began to tell their constituents that while they might work in Washington, they were not a part of the Washington establishment. They were independent thinkers. They understood the needs of the people back home. In short, they were avowed Washington outsiders.

Being an outsider does not depend on where one lives or works. One can live and work in Washington and still be a Washington outsider. Rather, it is a way of looking at government (see Kernell 1997: 42). Does one approve of big government? Does one believe that the people back home are capable of making decisions about their own lives, or should those decisions be made by faceless bureaucrats in giant, impersonal Washington-based agencies? Being a Washington outsider has much to do with anti-Washington rhetoric, not whether one is actually a part of the Washington establishment. After all, whether you want to call it the Washington establishment or not, membership in that exclusive club still remains a primary objective of many politicians.

By its very definition, then, the Washington outsider image is a blur; oftentimes it is a mere public relations gimmick. Politicians who have lived and worked in Washington for decades still maintain that they are really Washington outsiders. Perhaps the best example of the use of this image was former Tennessee Governor Lamar Alexander's 1996 bid for the Republican nomination. He proudly wore a plaid flannel shirt to his campaign events, a tangible symbol of his outsider status. The image, however, ran contrary to the fact that he had been George Bush's Secretary of Education, a position that would appear to be at the core of the Washington establishment. Another ultimate insider, businessman Ross Perot, who had lobbied President Richard Nixon from deep inside the Washington establishment, presented himself in 1992 and 1996 as an outsider. As these examples demonstrate, the distinction between insiders and outsiders is often unclear.

In contrast, being a Washington insider and cultivating the image of the master politician was, even in the Nixon years, clearly and directly tied to substantive policy making. FDR did not become known as a master politician simply because his image makers said he was one. His many substantive policy accomplishments were evidence of his political prowess. Likewise, Harry Truman had numerous substantive accomplishments in foreign affairs, although many were not recognized until years later. While the Eisenhower presidency represented a calm break from activist government and the Kennedy years were more style than substance, the Johnson presidency gave us the Great Society and civil rights legislation, while Nixon's presidency gave us environmental and occupational safety and health legislation, an opening to mainland China, and détente with the Soviet Union. In sum, real substantive accomplishments were associated with the presidents who adopted the image of the president as master politician. But as we shall argue, over time the line between substance and style has blurred until it has become difficult to determine one from the other. How did this happen?

Clearly, it began with Nixon's innovations in public relations (see Chapter 3). But there is more to the answer than this. As previously noted, Jimmy Carter cultivated the image of a common man presidency. But he also popularized a second image that has proven to be more enduring: the Washington outsider image. As Gary Rose (1997: 73) noted, "Carter's populist themes resonated with the voters, who, in the aftermath of Watergate, were attracted by the image of an honest outsider from Plains, Georgia." In fact, the "outsider route to the White House" had "become commonplace since [Senator Eugene] McCarthy's 1968" race for the Democratic nomination (Kernell 1985: 135). George Wallace then popularized anti-Washington rhetoric in his 1968 third-party presidential campaign. In 1972 Nixon co-opted much of Wallace's political agenda, including his anti-Washington rhetoric. Carter in 1976, Reagan in 1980 and 1984, and Clinton in 1992 then actively cultivated the Washington outsider image in their campaigns for the presidency. Presidential contenders as varied as Ross Perot, Lamar Alexander, Steve Forbes, Pat Buchanan, Michael Dukakis, and even the ultimate Washington insider, Bob Dole, also ran for president using this historical presidential image. Dole's use of the image is perhaps the most astounding. When it was apparent that he had secured his party's nomination for president, Dole, a long-time Washington insider, resigned from the Senate, then declared that his roots were really in Russell, Kansas, not Washington, D.C.! He transformed himself into Citizen Dole, not Senator Dole. Dole's attempt at image manipulation did not succeed, but former Hollywood star Ronald Reagan and the quintessential politician, Bill Clinton, who at another time in history might have been more comfortable cultivating the master politician image, were able to successfully convince the public that they were indeed Washington Outsiders. In fact, of the four presidents who followed Gerald Ford into the White House, only one, George Bush, did not run as a Washington outsider, although like his predecessor, Ronald Reagan, he did regularly stress anti-Washington themes in his campaign rhetoric.

The irony is that while more candidates are running as Washington outsiders, the image may not be a useful one in preparing a modern president for office. As Samuel Kernell (1997: 44) has written, "Fresh from an extended and successful stint of campaigning, an outsider will enter the White House probably as uninterested in playing the bargaining game as he is ill prepared" for it. Furthermore, if one is an actual Washington Outsider, with little experience in Washington, as Carter was, the problem is even greater. As Judith Michaels (1997: 285) has noted, "Whether . . . [outsiders] come in as new presidents, representatives, senators, or appointees, political newcomers to Washington . . . do not really know how the federal government works, how slow or convoluted is its movement. Their cocksure approach and self-confidence are quickly eroded and can turn into disillusionment and cynicism when faced repeatedly with political reality." Gary Rose (1997: 78) has added, "In an age of distrust of politicians, the political outsider can win the presidency—but, unfortunately, the outsider cannot govern."

This statement certainly describes Jimmy Carter's orientation into Washington politics. Carter was an unabashed Washington outsider. In his memoirs he says, "We came to Washington outsiders . . . we left as outsiders"; one entire section of his memoirs is boldly titled "An Outsider in Washington" (Carter 1982). Yet, much of his failure as president can be attributed to his lack of Washington experience and to the image of the outsider that he actively cultivated. He did not know how to play the Washington game. His campaign for president left him without a basis for trusting other Washington politicians, and they never came to trust him. Finally, had he any inclination to play the political game, he did not know how to bargain with others inside the Beltway. In summary, Carter's Washington outsider status virtually guaranteed that he would have serious problems governing once he arrived there.

There are, then, vast differences between the image of president as master politician and the image of the president as a Washington outsider. When presidents govern as insiders, they need to have close relations with other individuals inside the Beltway; that is, they need to know the temper of the town. But, when presidents govern as outsiders, connections with insiders are a perceived liability and the opinion of the broader public outside of Washington takes on greater importance. Likewise, as Kernell (1997: 46) has commented, "A president who developed his political skills in the chambers and corridors of Congress will understandably find it exasperating to deliver salutations to a television camera." For the outsider, however, television becomes a critical tool to cultivate public opinion. If a president cannot influence Washington insiders, then his or her only major resource for political power will be public opinion.

It is probably no coincidence then that every president since Jimmy Carter has maintained pollsters in the White House whose job it is to continuously—sometimes weekly, sometimes daily—monitor the public's opinion. During 1993 the Clinton administration averaged 3 or 4 polls and 3 and 4 focus groups per month (Kernell 1997: 35). For presidents who try to govern outside the system, such constant polling is of vital importance. The trouble is that as polling becomes more and more pervasive, it becomes difficult to determine whether presidents are leading public opinion or being led by it. Furthermore, this pattern encourages presidents to speak more often in order to reach out to the public. But as we will argue in Chapter 5, speaking more often is not the same thing as saying more. Finally, in a poll-driven age, images become more transitory. As style becomes more important than substance, images become dispensable, a point we will return to in the next chapter.

Conclusions

In this chapter we have examined the transformation of historical presidential images over time. We have found that certain images tend to be more acceptable at certain periods in American history and less so at other times. For example, the common man image was of great value to presidents in the nineteenth century. Individuals as diverse as Andrew Jackson, Abraham Lincoln, and William Henry Harrison associated themselves with this image. Early in the twentieth century the common man image was still successfully employed by Calvin Coolidge. Once Franklin Roosevelt redefined the presidency, however, the common man image became a double-edged sword. It might help to elevate an individual to the White House, but it also reminded the public that a particular individual was not big enough for the job. Harry Truman, Gerald Ford, and Jimmy Carter were all perceived to be too ordinary to be president. Of these presidents, only Truman overcame this handicap, though it dogged him to his last day as president. And while Dwight Eisenhower did not run from the common man image, his heroic image inoculated him from the charge that he was not a big enough man for the job. Since Carter, no president has embraced the common man image.

The common man image was replaced by the master politician image, which was primarily the product of the two Roosevelts. This image is tied inextricably to governance. In order to be a master politician a president has to demonstrate that he or she actually has substantive accomplishments. The presidencies of Franklin Roosevelt, Truman (who was able to cultivate this image in foreign affairs), Johnson, and Nixon are thus replete with major substantive accomplishments. As television became more pervasive and intrusive, and as the Washington political community became less amenable to a bargaining presidency, the master politician image fell into disrepute. Certainly, Johnson and Nixon contributed the most to the image's decline. They also opened the door for a third historical presidential image.

The Washington outsider is the prevalent image of the moment. Carter, Reagan, and Clinton have embraced it. Almost all politicians now sound anti-Washington rhetoric as well. The problem with the Washington outsider image is that it is much less compatible with governance than was the president as master politician image. This is so in part because the kind of individuals who will successfully adopt this image are less skilled in the art of Washington politics. They also are more likely to see public speaking as integral to the presidency and less likely to engage in bargaining with Washington insiders.

As we shall see in the next chapter, as public relations has made its way to the forefront of American politics, personal presidential images have become ever more transitory, and substance more often than not has become a mere prop for image creation. There is a reason for this. In an age when perceptions are of primary importance, substance actually can have deleterious consequences. Appearing to be successful may therefore be a more useful strategy than achieving actual policy success. As we shall argue, the central dilemma for the presidency today is that image politics encourages presidents to put style before substance.

3

Personal Images

May not an ass know when the cart draws the horse?

—Spoken by "The Fool" in Shakespeare's *King Lear*,
Act I, Scene IV

John and Jackie Kennedy playing tennis on their honeymoon in Hyannis, June 1955.
Photo courtesy of Archive Photos, reprinted with permission.

In Chapter 2 we examined three historical images that presidents have adopted throughout American history. In adopting an image or images, presidents also attach themselves to certain symbols and imagery conducive to that image. For example, common man presidents have adopted symbols such as log cabins to show that they are indeed one of us. Master politician presidents have invoked images of action. Washington outsider presidents and presidential candidates have adopted such varied symbols as plaid shirts or an airplane named "Citizen Dole" to show us they are not really part of the Washington establishment. In sum, many symbols are associated with the three broad historical images we examined in the last chapter.

In addition to the three historical images, however, presidents also adopt personal images. These images relate to the personality of the individual president or presidential candidate, as well as to the specific political needs of a particular administration. These needs may change; for example, if there is an international crisis, a president may be forced to adopt more belligerent images in order to convince the American public he or she is strong on national defense. Statistics likewise may indicate that the public is becoming more concerned about the nation's poor. A president now needs to associate himself or herself with more caring and compassionate images. As a consequence, personal images tend to be much more transitory than historical images, and are therefore more disposable. If one image doesn't fit a president or presidential candidate particularly well, then an image makeover is in order. If Richard Nixon, for example, developed an image as a "loser" (for having lost the 1960 presidential campaign and the 1962 California governor's race), or if he was seen as a bit too mean-spirited, then create a "New Nixon," as his campaign team did in 1968.

The creation of personal images is generally a team effort. Beginning with Nixon, whom we refer to as the first image-is-everything president, presidents have surrounded themselves with pollsters, political consultants, and other professionals whose job it is to portray them in the best possible light. The result is that for many of our most recent presidents policy substance has become a mere prop for image making. Political consultants sometimes even convince presidents to adopt a particular policy or even a broad agenda in order to promote a desired personal image. To demonstrate how this has been done, in this chapter we first discuss John Kennedy, an early advocate of image politics, and then examine the personal images of four presidents—Richard Nixon, Ronald Reagan, George Bush, and Bill Clinton.

John Kennedy: Image Versus Reality

Throughout his presidency John F. Kennedy was an extraordinarily popular president. His approval ratings generally fell into the 60 and 70 percent range (Raichur and Waterman 1993). Even over thirty years after his assassination, he continues to be remarkably popular. In a poll conducted in January and February of 1996 by the University of New Mexico's Institute for Public Policy (another part of which is discussed in Chapter 1), 574 respondents were asked to retrospectively evaluate the perceived performance of eight former presidents plus the incumbent, Bill Clinton. Respondents were asked to use the following scale: excellent, good, fair, or poor. Kennedy's performance was classified as "excellent" by 29.7 percent of the respondents, a higher percentage than given any other president. Eisenhower was second at 21 percent. Only 6.4 percent classified Clinton's performance as "excellent." Of the poll's respondents, 46.3 percent classified Kennedy's performance as "good," second only to Eisenhower's 50.2 percent. Only 3.9 percent ranked Kennedy's performance as "poor." When the nine presidents were rank ordered by a combination of the "excellent" and "good" responses, Kennedy ranked first at 76.0 percent. The others were ranked as follows: Eisenhower 71.2 percent, George Bush 59.2 percent, Ronald Reagan 54.5 percent, Jimmy Carter 37.7 percent, Lyndon Johnson 36.5 percent, Gerald Ford 35.6 percent, Clinton 34.2 percent, and Richard Nixon 32.9 percent.

It is clear, then, that public perceptions of Kennedy remain highly favorable. But Kennedy's record of accomplishment was actually rather meager. It can be argued that his foreign and domestic policy accomplishments were relatively few. His presidency virtually commenced with the Bay of Pigs disaster. The Vienna Conference with Khrushchev was likewise perceived by Kennedy's contemporaries as a failure, and encouraged the Soviets to proceed with the construction of the Berlin Wall. International tensions increased over Berlin, and a tangible fear that the Southeast Asian nation of Laos would soon be lost to the Communists, contributed to Kennedy's very checkered foreign policy record prior to the Cuban Missile Crisis. Some historians have argued that had not the Kremlin perceived Kennedy as being weak, Khrushchev would likely never have committed nuclear weapons to Cuba in the first place. For example, Michael Riccards (1995: Vol. 2, 273) has written, "[in that crisis] Kennedy was worried about more than the strategic balance; he was also concerned about personally appearing to look weak and ineffectual once again. That political fear was so profound that he was willing in the end to risk nuclear war rather than face that threat to his image and self-concept." In a recent book highly critical of the Kennedy presidency, Seymour Hersh (1997) has advanced a similar argument. Other evidence, particularly the recently released White House tapes of the unfolding crisis (see May and Zelikow 1997) support the more traditional view that the Missile Crisis was indeed Kennedy's greatest moment as president. Taken as a whole, though, and including his movement of additional troops into Vietnam, Kennedy's foreign policy record is not impressive.

His domestic policy record is likewise sparse. His greatest achievements were his call to land a man on the moon before the end of the 1960s, to create the Peace Corps, and to propose a tax cut (which was passed after his death). He also introduced civil rights legislation that, again, would be passed after his death. While he is generally given broad credit for the last-named legislation, Kennedy was not highly motivated by the civil rights cause. Rather, he had hesitated on the issue, fearing the loss of southern support. His decision to send legislation to Congress reflected as much his brother Robert Kennedy's advocacy and transpiring events that simply could no longer be ignored as it did a palpable commitment to the cause by the president himself. In summary, a case can be made that John Kennedy's domestic policy record was sparse indeed, particularly in comparison to other presidents who adopted the master politician image. Even if we acknowledge that Kennedy was unable to finish out his first term in office, he did serve nearly three years. In that time frame other presidents (for example, Teddy Roosevelt, Woodrow Wilson, Franklin Roosevelt, Lyndon Johnson, Richard Nixon, Bill Clinton) certainly had a more impressive record of accomplishment than did Kennedy. Why then was he so popular at the time and why does he continue to receive extraordinarily high levels of popular support?

It is clear that what we most remember today is not the Bay of Pigs disaster or the Vienna Conference or even the Missile Crisis. What we most remember today are the images of a virile young president, speaking stridently to the nation about his upbeat vision of the future. We remember Kennedy's vitality. As Riccards (1995: Vol. 2, 273) noted, "All his adult life, Kennedy had cultivated a pose of courage and toughness." Those images stay with us even today, frozen in our minds, of course, by his assassination. Because he died young he was never allowed to age ungracefully, nor was he forced to confront the many allegations that he was a world-class womanizer or that his father helped him steal the 1960 election. What we remember of Kennedy is not the man himself, but the images of youth, wit, and intelligence and of Camelot that were so carefully and skillfully cultivated after his presidency by the men who had been closest to Kennedy throughout his life and political career (see, for example, *Johnny We Hardly Knew You*).

In addition, the full possibilities of a new type of pseudo-event, the presidential "spectacle," became apparent during Kennedy's presidency. As Bruce Miroff (1988: 277) has written, "Certainly there were precursors to Kennedy in this regard—especially the two Roosevelts—but the coming together of vast media coverage, inflated popular expectations, and talent at producing spectacle is first evident in the New Frontier." Miroff continued, Kennedy's presidency "would be" one "that projected youth, vigor, and novelty, that recast the institution itself as a headquarters for intelligence and masterful will." In showing us the power of images, John Fitzgerald Kennedy thus provided a powerful lesson for his successors. This lesson was not lost on the man who had been defeated by Kennedy in 1960—Richard Milhous Nixon.

Richard Nixon: The Creation of the Image-Is-Everything Presidency

With the memory of Camelot firmly fixed in his mind, it is not surprising that Richard Nixon was concerned, some might even argue obsessed, with presidential image making. His use of campaign personnel to carefully craft a desirable image (see Chapter 4) and his establishment of new White House institutions charged with crafting and perpetuating a favorable presidential image lead us to refer to Nixon as the first image-is-everything president. The ultimate irony is that despite all of his attempts at image creation, Richard Nixon is now remembered as a corrupt politician who lied to Congress and to the American people.

In addition to being the first image-is-everything president, Nixon was also the last president (to date) to covet the historical master politician image. As such, his presidency represents a bridge between the politics of the past and the politics of the present, in which television would play a major role.

Unlike his immediate predecessor, Lyndon Johnson, Richard Nixon was keenly aware of the power of television. In his memoirs, Nixon (1978: 354) wrote,

> Since the advent of television as our primary means of communication and source of information modern Presidents must have specialized talents at once more superficial and more complicated than those of their predecessors. They must try to master the art of manipulating the media not only to win in politics but in order to further the programs and causes they believe in; at the same time they must avoid at all costs the charge of trying to manipulate the media. In the modern presidency, concern for image must rank with concern for substance . . .

While Nixon understood the importance of images, he was not particularly pleased with its relationship to substance. He continued, "I do not like this situation; I can remember a time in American politics when it was not the case. But today it is a fact of life, and anyone who seeks a position of influence in politics must cope with it; anyone who seeks a position of leadership must master it."

Because he disliked image making, Nixon "kicked, bucked and dragged his feet when" his White House aides "suggested he get up from his desk and venture forth among the people" (Ehrlichman 1982: 242). Despite his dislike, however, he clearly understood the importance of such activities in promoting the president's image and agenda. One of Nixon's top White House aides, John Ehrlichman, has written, "Richard Nixon . . . seemed to believe there was no national issue that was not susceptible to public relations treatment" (ibid., 248). Thus, when Arthur Burns, presidential adviser on economics, produced a pessimistic report on the state of the economy, Nixon's response was: "We need a media campaign about the economy" (ibid., 249).

But the problem with public relations is that "trust and accurate information play a decreasing role. The details of policy become deemphasized" and what "a president does becomes significantly less important than how he or she does it" (Stuckey 1991: 83). By adopting public relations responses to, for instance, an economic problem, the president was devaluing substance and replacing it with symbolism. As political scientist Mary Stuckey (1991: 89) commented,

> The focus on public relations to the exclusion of specific policy had clear—and clearly negative—consequences. Harry Truman could say, "Make good policies, and good relations with the people will follow." Nixon seemed to believe that if he could "make" good relations with the American people, he would then be free to make good policy.

In other words, as early as the Nixon presidency, *the public relations cart had already been placed ahead of the policy horse.* Image was becoming more important than policy substance. Throughout his presidency Nixon remained concerned with his image. Diary notes from H. R. Haldeman, his Chief of Staff, for February 2, 1970, noted that Nixon identified the "need for better press" in order to promote the president's "image and leadership." He said that all of the background information the administration provided to the press dealt with what the administration had accomplished, with nothing about the personality of the president himself (Haldeman 1994: 125). Nixon then reminded Haldeman that John Kennedy did nothing while he was president "but appeared great; LBJ did everything but appeared terrible." William Howard Taft was "infinitely more effective than Teddy Roosevelt." Yet "Roosevelt had personality. Taft just did well." John

Ehrlichman (1982: 240) noted this same exchange in his memoirs. Nixon's message to Haldeman and Ehrlichman, his two top advisers, was clear. It isn't merely accomplishments that mark a president as a success or failure, but how that president's message is communicated and how it is perceived by the American people.

To actively craft a favorable image and to handle the press, Nixon created the Office of Communications in the White House. He understood that communicating a carefully selected message was of critical importance in the modern presidency. Ehrlichman (1982: 239) has estimated "that Richard Nixon spent half his working time on the nonsubstantive aspects of the Presidency, and probably 40 percent of that half dealing with the problems of communication." Ehrlichman continued, "I recognize that a good argument can be made that communication is the substance of the Presidency. But from where I sat, [Treasury Secretary] George Shultz, [National Security Adviser] Henry Kissinger, and I were dealing in substance—policy and its implementation—while Bob Haldeman's element of the staff was concerned with process and appearances."

Haldeman, himself, had what might at first glance appear to be a rather unusual background for a president's Chief of Staff. He was a former advertising man who had risen to prominence by launching a television show called "I Search for Adventure" (Haldeman and DiMona 1978: 480). As Chief of Staff, Haldeman played a major role in crafting the president's image. When Nixon visited Berlin, for example, the president was concerned that the crowds for his public appearance might be compared unfavorably to those Kennedy had generated when he had visited Berlin. Haldeman ensured large crowds by having traffic blocked on nearby streets, then spreading the word that the president of the United States would be passing by on a nearby avenue. Through this subterfuge Nixon was guaranteed large crowds and favorable press coverage.

For all of his public relations efforts, however, Nixon was never able to ameliorate the negative image the American public had of him. He was, after all, a politician in an age when the word *politics* was increasingly taking on a negative connotation. Hence, at the height of the Watergate scandal, when the White House tried to humanize the president by having the press photograph Nixon as he walked in solitude on a lonely beach, it was the fact that he was wearing a suit and expensive shoes that made headlines the next day. Even in a moment of relaxation or contemplation, Nixon was seen as a typical politician.

Given Nixon's preoccupation with image it is indeed ironic that he is now remembered, not for his substantive accomplishments (of which there were many in both foreign and domestic affairs, certainly more than Kennedy had), but for his various Watergate-related activities. Haldeman commented on this irony, "Just as he who lives by the sword must die by the sword, so he whose image or public perception is based on inaccurate overbalancing of his good qualities must be brought down by the revelation of flaws in that imbalanced portrayal" (Haldeman and DiMona 1978: 324). The motto of the Nixon presidency may very well be, then, that those who live by the image shall die by the image. Still, Nixon's problems could legitimately be blamed on his own personality flaws and not with the image-is-everything approach. Consequently, while Nixon's successors would decry his ethics, they would adopt his image-creating practices.

Ronald Reagan: The "Ultimate Media President"

As we have noted, Richard Nixon, the last of the presidents to cultivate and govern under the president-as-master-politician image, was also the first president to adopt the tools of the image-is-everything presidency (for example, extensive use of public relations). Ronald Reagan appointed many former Nixon officials to his own administration. Among the skills they brought with them were their experience at image making and manipulation. In addition, Reagan brought his own talented image makers to the White House, most notably Michael Deaver, who would become one-third of Reagan's White House "Troika." It is therefore not surprising that Reagan's presidency, like Nixon's, was dominated by public relations efforts, polling, focus groups, media manipulation, and other attempts at image control.

Reagan was in fact an image maker's dream come true, a former actor who became "the ultimate media president" (Riccards 1995: Vol. 2, 344). Riccards noted that Reagan accomplished this objective "by substituting images for ideas." From the very beginning of his presidency, Reagan's image makers carefully crafted public perceptions of the president in order to increase his personal popularity, even if the public did not agree with him on specific policy stances. Michael Deaver, his chief image maker, was largely uninterested in policy. When Reagan's first Chief of Staff, James Baker, tried to involve him in the substance of policy making, Deaver refused (Deaver 1987: 135). Deaver was more interested in creating a proper image of his president. His ultimate tool was television. Deaver (1987: 73) strongly believed that "in the television age, image sometimes is as useful as substance. Not as important, but as useful" (ibid., 73).

Deaver had two basic rules for surviving Washington politics: "1) You must believe that what you are doing is more important than you and your personal needs; and 2) you must not confuse the image with the reality" (ibid., 140). This second point was of particular importance, because, according to Deaver, there was a disjuncture between Reagan's public image and the stark reality of his personal life. As Deaver stated,

> To most Americans, the Reagans remain a symbol of family values, so the polls tell us. The image does not quite square with the record. This is our first divorced president, a father who has suffered his share of rebellious children. Although only an occasional churchgoer, he has touched us on a spiritual level—more so than Jimmy Carter, who was as close to as this country has come to putting a preacher in the White House. (ibid., 101)

With regard to the latter image, Reagan biographer Wilbur Edel (1992: 1) noted, "The most striking aspect of Ronald Reagan's political career is his fundamentalist religious approach to public service." Edel noted "Reagan's practice of concluding every speech or public appearance with a religious reference or appeal." (ibid., 3). These public utterances gave the impression that he was a deeply religious man. As Deaver reminds us, while Reagan was personally religious, he was only an occasional churchgoer. Reagan's rhetoric, however, was sufficient to overcome charges that he did not always practice what he preached.

Reagan also had an image as a man who stood tall and tough. Yet as Deaver (1987: 177) has noted, "Ronald Reagan never left the American shores during World War II. He never left Hollywood, where he served as a captain in what was then known as the Army Air Corps." Reagan's job was to make training films in Culver City, California. Hence, while it was important for Deaver not to "confuse the image with the reality," that appears to have been his primary job. It should be noted, however, that Deaver appears to have been troubled by this role (ibid., 150–151):

> As a so-called image maker, I am torn between thinking about how I can best take advantage of this trend, and where it is likely to lead us. It is not hard to picture a scenario not unlike *The Dating Game*, where three candidates give their qualifications, smile, and answer questions about how old they were when they were allowed to car-date, and the studio audience presses a button indicating their favorite.

In his memoirs, one gets the sense that Deaver (175) is trying to justify his role as the president's image maker when he writes, "When you get down to it, it is people that make a presidency work, not images." But then he is compelled to add, "But images help."

Reagan regularly invoked images throughout his presidency. He became the master of what Daniel Boorstin called in Chapter 1 the "pseudo-event." Most of these events were highly successful, particularly those related to world politics. As his principal biographer, Lou Cannon (1992: 458) wrote, "Ronald Reagan's talents as a performer were suited to the world stage. His writers lavished their finest scripts and his White House impresarios their most elaborate productions on Reagan's appearances in London, Normandy, Korea, Moscow, and at the Berlin

Wall." As Michael Deaver (1987: 141) noted, when Reagan "surveyed the Normandy coast, or the Demilitarized Zone between North and South Korea, you had a sense of sweep and panorama that any [film] director must feel. And it is in this kind of environment that Ronald Reagan did more than star. He glowed."

The visit to Normandy Beach, on the 40th anniversary of the D-Day landing, was particularly memorable. White House political consultants spent months picking out exactly the right camera angle and background for his speech. When Reagan delivered the address, the American public saw their president standing before one of the most extraordinary vistas in the history of presidential speech-making. The impression thus derived was that Reagan and America were still standing tall, not that Reagan had been making movies in Hollywood instead of storming the Normandy beaches.

Reagan also mixed pseudo-events with policy making. It can be argued that the U.S. military invasion of Grenada was a pseudo-event. The invasion was of very limited military value; the main military justification was that an airport being constructed on the island could be used to transport supplies into other Central American nations threatened by communism. It turned out that the airport was being constructed to promote tourism and that it was too small to accommodate planes capable of transporting large quantities of goods to other nations. The real importance of the invasion was not military, but the signal it sent the American people. America was back. America would not tolerate a communist government in its own backyard. The invasion of Grenada fortified Reagan's popular standing, particularly in the southern states, and solidified his personal image as a tough president. Reagan used other symbols to promote this image, such as his cowboy attire and pictures of him chopping wood at his ranch in California. But not every pseudo-event was successful. For example, in 1985 German Chancellor Helmut Kohl wanted to schedule a joint ceremony with Reagan designed to repair his nation's tattered reputation from World War II. As Reagan (1990: 380) later wrote in his memoirs, "I didn't think it was right to keep on punishing every German for the Holocaust, including generations not yet born in the time of Hitler." The ceremony they planned, however, would turn out not to transmit the desired image.

The plan was for the two leaders to visit a cemetery in Bitburg, Germany. Unfortunately, what no one realized when the ceremony was planned was that a small number of SS officers were buried in that cemetery. This revelation produced a storm of protest over the proposed presidential visit. A new and unwanted image of the president—as for example, a callous man who did not care about the suffering of the victims of World War II—suddenly emerged. To deal with this image problem, the White House scheduled a visit to one of the death camps, to pay homage to the victims of Germany's genocidal policy against the

Jews. This visit, of course, further undercut the original purpose of the Bitburg visit, which had been to repair Germany's reputation from World War II. The result of this pseudo-event fiasco was to call Reagan's image into question and for several days the television news shows portrayed a White House under siege—not the image the White House desired. This example demonstrates that even carefully planned pseudo-events can have unintended consequences.

For the most part, however, Reagan was the master of the pseudo-event and of image creation. Most often, when other politicians attempted to create less flattering counterimages to use against Reagan, they were not successful. For example, according to Deaver (1987: 97), during the 1980 campaign Jimmy Carter tried to make Reagan look like a "warmonger." This attempt failed because those people "who shared this fear were reassured by Reagan's words and benign television manner. For millions of others, the image of an itchy trigger finger was no liability. They were weary of seeing America pushed around." As a result, "Reagan had it both ways."

Negative images of Reagan did emerge, however. For example, Reagan developed the well-deserved image of a detached president who did not know what his own administration was doing. This image began to appear when it was reported that Reagan had not recognized his own Secretary of Housing and Urban Development, Samuel Pierce, at a meeting with U.S. mayors. It was also revealed that he fell asleep in a meeting with the pope, as well as at Cabinet meetings. Later, his wife Nancy was caught on camera giving him the answer to a reporter's question. "We're doing the best we can," she whispered. Reagan then turned to the reporter and repeated, "We're doing the best we can." In his news conferences, Reagan regularly made comments like, "They don't want me to talk about this." Who "they" were was never explained. Finally, when Chief of Staff James Baker and Treasury Secretary Donald Regan decided to switch jobs, they brought the idea to the president. Reagan did not seem concerned. In fact, he didn't even ask a single policy-related question. He simply smiled and approved the deal (see Regan 1988). Could anyone imagine Richard Nixon or Lyndon Johnson doing such a thing?

Yet, despite all this evidence, all of which was well known during his presidency, the charge that Reagan was out of touch did not stick. So resilient was Reagan against such negative images that Democratic Congresswoman Patricia Schroeder called him "the Teflon President," because nothing ever seemed to stick to him. When Reagan's distracted performance in the first debate with Walter Mondale in 1984 led the respected *Wall Street Journal* to raise questions about Reagan's age and competence, Reagan deflected criticism by joking about his age; he would not make his opponent's youth and inexperience an issue in the campaign. America laughed, and the image of Reagan as too old or too detached to be an effective president faded from memory.

These negative images only resurfaced after the details of the Iran-Contra scandal were exposed. Suddenly there was overwhelming evidence that Reagan was indeed detached from the daily business of his own administration. Yet, even the Iran-Contra revelations did not destroy his presidency. While his image for toughness (especially with terrorists) was damaged, it was not destroyed. He continued to be a popular president until he retired from the White House in January of 1989.

George Bush: Dueling Images

Reagan's successor, George Herbert Walker Bush, was less successful in controlling his image, or in presenting a consistent image to the American public. One of the primary problems with image politics is that images oftentimes do not reflect reality. Because they are related to perceptions and perceptions can change, images change as well. George Bush is a perfect example of a president who had multiple and conflicting images. Bush's first significant public image was that of the loyal vice president. When he ran for president in 1980, Bush differentiated himself from his political opponent, Ronald Reagan, by characterizing Reagan's economic proposal as "voodoo economics." Yet in July 1980, when he was offered the vice presidential nomination, Bush quickly jettisoned any sign of disagreement with Reagan's economic plan. From this point onward he actively cultivated the image of the loyal vice president, unwilling under any circumstances to disagree with his president. As Jack Germond and Jules Witcover (1989: 73) have written, even as he prepared to run for office on his own in 1988, "Anytime there was the slightest public perception that Bush might be getting out of step with his benefactor, the vice president quickly rectified or blurred it." His desire was to remain "Reagan's loyal servant."

His eight years in the vice presidency led to the development of a highly unflattering image of George Bush. In a 1987 cover story, *Newsweek* magazine proclaimed that if he was to seek the White House in 1988, George Bush would have to first deal with the "Wimp Factor." Bush was personally outraged by this story, but the wimp image stuck. The contrast between the president and vice president could not be made any clearer. While Reagan was perceived as tough, his vice president, George Bush, was considered weak. Clearly, if Bush was to win the presidency he would have to replace the wimp factor image with a tough public image.

To accomplish this objective, his advisers decided to adopt a more aggressive campaign style for their candidate. The genesis of this new image strategy was to come during a live network television interview with Dan Rather on *CBS Evening News*. Prior to the interview, Bush's campaign advisers told their candidate that he was being set up by Rather and that CBS News was going to blindside him by asking him harsh questions about his involvement in the Iran-Contra affair. The live Bush interview was preceded by a nearly five-minute filmed story about the affair. "As Bush watched on the monitor in his office, he grew visibly angry . . ." (ibid., 121), which is precisely what his staff wanted. Once the interview commenced, Bush stridently attacked Rather, even reminding viewers that the news anchor had let the television screen go black for several minutes at the beginning of a recent news broadcast, a cardinal sin in the television news business. "The public reaction was almost immediate—and one-sided against Rather" (ibid., 124). Suddenly, candidate Bush had a new image. To fortify the new image, the campaign targeted issues designed to make their candidate look tough, for example, capital punishment. As George Bush called for the death penalty the image was clear: This man is not a wimp.

This effort at image manipulation worked, to a certain extent. Unfortunately, another negative image of George Bush developed along with his new, more strident one. Back in 1984, following the 1984 vice presidential debate with Geraldine Ferraro, Bush had triumphantly declared that he had "kicked a little ass last night." The comment had been seen as crass and as evidence that George Bush was perfectly capable of clutching defeat from the jaws of victory. Now, in 1988, the day after his televised confrontation with Dan Rather, Bush told a campaign audience in Cody, Wyoming, "It's tension city when you're in there" (ibid., 125). As in 1984, his comment deflected attention away from the previous day's success. Such comments, along with Bush's propensity to use a bizarre syntax all his own, ultimately contributed to a new and unwanted image: George Bush as silly politician. Comedian Dana Carvey would translate this new image into a regular feature on the TV program *Saturday Night Live*. Unfortunately for George Bush, no matter what image his campaign tried to create, the image of the silly politician never faded from the public's consciousness.

Compounding Bush's problems was the fact that he had articulated no commanding vision for the American people in 1988, or later during his presidency. Falling back into the silly politician persona, he even provided comedians with a solid one-liner when he stated that he lacked the "vision thing." As a result, Bush's promises raised the art of empty rhetoric to new heights. In his speech before the 1988 Republican Convention, he promised "a kinder and gentler America," he passionately extolled the nation to look forward to "a thousand points of light," and he promised to be both the nation's "Education President" and its "Environmental President." Yet he provided no clear idea of what he meant by any of these terms. Each sounded good, at least good enough to get him elected, but they did not easily translate into policy. What did Bush mean by "a kinder and gentler America"? Kinder and gentler than what? The policies of his predecessor, Ronald Reagan? What did he mean by "a thousand points of light"? It referred to the spirit of volunteerism nationwide, but in his speech he didn't shed any light on what his administration would do to promote volunteerism. As the nation's "Education President," George Bush did not propose any bold initiatives, nor did he seek significant increases in funding for education. Only as the "Environmental President" did Bush ultimately make a major contribution: passage of the Clean Air Act of 1990. But on the very same day that the president signed this legislation, his top legal adviser in the White House was working to find ways around the legislation's major provisions. Later, Vice President Dan Quayle's Council on Competitiveness would be accused of holding secret backroom meetings with the regulated industry in an attempt to undercut the legislation's implementation. In short, George Bush's campaign rhetoric did not translate into a substantive record of achievement as president. The "vision thing" would continue to be an image problem throughout his presidency.

To deal with the silly politician, "vision thing," and wimp images, the Bush campaign made what ultimately proved to be a fateful mistake. Of all of George Bush's 1988 campaign statements, none would be as well remembered as his promise at the Republican Convention: "Read my lips; no new taxes"; and no campaign promise would cause him more grief. The "read my lips" pledge is an example of a carefully staged and crafted attempt at image manipulation, but one that ultimately went awry.

At the 1988 Republican Convention George Bush was preparing to give what many political pundits were calling the speech of his lifetime. Peggy Noonan (1990: 298), who was the primary author of the speech, noted, "In June we hadn't known . . . [the speech] would be so important, but then [Democratic nominee Michael] Dukakis gave his speech, and the Democrats came out of their convention fourteen points ahead, and suddenly the acceptance speech was crucial."

The task ahead for George Bush was formidable. He had to convince both conservatives within his own party and the American public that he was worthy of inheriting the Ronald Reagan legacy. To accomplish that it was decided he had to seize on one fundamental issue dear to the hearts of conservatives and popular with the public. According to Noonan (1990: 307), "Jack Kemp told me, Hit [sic] hard on taxes, Bush will be pressured to make clear he won't budge." From this conversation emerged the most famous and controversial passage of George

Bush's acceptance speech. The Republican nominee would say, "The Congress will push me to raise taxes, and I'll say no, and they'll push me, and I'll say no, and they'll push again. And all I can say to them is read my lips: No New Taxes."

According to political reporters Michael Duffy and Dan Goodgame (1992: 31), the tax pledge proved to be instrumental in winning over the support of independent suburbanites, a critical component of the Reagan coalition. But this passage proved controversial even prior to its delivery to the Republican Convention. While such campaign luminaries as Peggy Noonan and Roger Ailes favored its inclusion, pollster Robert Teeter and top legislative strategist Richard Darman sharply objected, pointing out that the passage would diminish Bush's capacity to govern once he was elected. They vehemently warned that the tax pledge would almost certainly have to be broken and when that happened, it would severely damage the new president's credibility (Skowronek 1993: 437). But according to presidential scholar Stephen Skowronek (ibid., 437), Noonan and Ailes "were concerned primarily with the dramatic structure of the campaign, with creating the appropriate images, and with casting Bush in the most authentic light possible in the moment at hand. They argued that, more than anything else, Bush needed to sharpen his image."

In the end the image makers were victorious and the "read my lips" pledge remained in the speech. It helped to get George Bush elected, but right from the beginning of his administration, top economic advisers struggled to find a way to break the promise without seeming to do so. By choosing image over substance in his acceptance speech, Bush had effectively shackled his economic team. Edward Rollins (1996: 205), the head of the National Republican Congressional Committee, told Robert Teeter in 1990 that if the president violated his tax pledge "you are going to get killed. This is the most sacred pledge he made. If you raise taxes in this term, he can kiss his ass away in '92, and he's going to take a bunch of House members with him." Despite such warnings, on June 26, 1990, the president approved a bipartisan statement that acknowledged that taxes must be raised to deal with the deficit. Democrats in Congress predictably accused the president of violating his "read my lips, no new taxes" pledge, while angry Republicans such as Representative Newt Gingrich said they would not vote for higher taxes. Three days later, the president told a press conference that he was ready to take the "slings and arrows" of criticism over his decision to raise taxes. But it was already too late for damage control. The *New York Times* headlined, "Bush Abandons Vow, Backs a Tax Increase." The *New York Post* was typically more acerbic with its headline: "Read My Lips—I Lied" (Duffy and Goodgame 1992: 236). According to Duffy and Goodgame (155) other papers ran words in their headlines such as "waffle, retreat, blink, and flip-flop." Meanwhile, the president's conservative base was outraged. As conservative Charles Kolb (1994: 56) would later write, "It was Bush's single biggest mistake as President, and it led directly to the unraveling of the Reagan coalition and Bush's eventual defeat." More immediately, the president's approval rating plunged by twenty points. While the Persian Gulf War would, for a time, divert the nation's attention away from the budget issue, the president's image as a tough politician willing to stand up to the Democrats in Congress had been shattered forever.

In its place a new presidential image formed: George Bush was a traditional politician who was willing to say anything to get elected, a devastating image in the era of the Washington Outsider. The president, perhaps inadvertently, promoted this new image in an interview with David Frost of the Public Broadcasting System on January 3, 1992. Bush told Frost, "I will do what I have to do to be reelected." It was this presidential image that George Bush took with him into his 1992 failed reelection campaign.

But Bush would develop yet one more image. He would have the ill fortune of running for reelection while the country was still experiencing the effects of what ultimately would prove to be a relatively short-lived recession. When his top advisers urged him to assuage the public's concerns about the recession, George Bush demurred. He told his advisers he would not say anything until his 1992 State of the Union address. Although much anticipated, the speech included few specifics and did little to mollify an increasingly angry electorate (Waterman 1996). In New Hampshire, campaigning in that state's presidential primary, Bush compounded matters. His campaign advisers asked him to say something about how much he cared about the concerns of ordinary Americans. They gave him an index card that simply read, "Message, I care." The president was supposed to improvise a statement about his concern over the economy. Instead, he merely repeated the phrase written on the index card. This action promoted two deleterious images at once: George Bush as the silly politician, and a new image, George Bush as the uncaring, out-of-touch-with-the-needs-of-ordinary-Americans president (the antithesis of the common man image).

On February 4, 1992, in Orlando, Florida, at the National Grocers Association convention, things got even worse for the president. He was photographed while watching a clerk operate an electronic pad used to identify forged checks. The president asked, "If some guy came in and spelled George Bush differently, could you catch it?" According to *New York Times* correspondent Andrew Rosenthal (2–5–92: A1), "'Yes,' he was told, and [the president] shook his head in wonder. Then he grabbed a quart of milk, a light bulb and a bag of candy and ran them over an electronic scanner. The look of wonder flickered across his face again as he saw the item and price registered on the cash register. 'This is for checking out?' asked Mr.

Bush. 'I just took a tour through the exhibits here,' he told the grocers later. 'Amazed by some of the technology.'" The incident proved embarrassing because the price scanner technology had been prevalent in grocery stores for many years. The incident underscored Bush's image as a rich man and professional politician who was out of touch with the lives of ordinary Americans. While the common man image no longer prevailed by the time of Bush's presidency, this incident suggests that presidents still have to be mindful of it. While presidents can no longer be perceived as too common, neither can they be perceived as too privileged.

The grocery scanner incident, as often happens in the age of pseudo-events, degenerated into a public relations contest. The press immediately asked the White House when was the last time the president had ever been in a grocery store. White House Press Secretary Marlin Fitzwater told reporters that he had seen the president visit a grocery store within the last year or so, in Kennebunkport, Maine. In fact, Mr. Bush had not done any grocery shopping in a number of years, except, that is, to buy an occasional item in a convenience store.

The issue was certainly silly, but it proved devastating to Bush's image. Later that year, in a question and answer session with ordinary Americans on *CBS This Morning*, a woman asked Bush's Democratic rival, Bill Clinton, how much a gallon of milk and a loaf of bread cost. Clinton answered the questions competently. The lesson of this exchange was clear: Bill Clinton was in touch with the concerns of ordinary Americans, while George Bush was not. Then, that fall, in the second presidential debate, Bush appeared confused when a woman asked him about the impact of the deficit on the lives of ordinary people. He stumbled, telling the woman that just because he didn't have cancer didn't mean that he couldn't feel empathy for someone who did. The exchange again promoted the image that George Bush was out of touch. What is sad about all of these exchanges is their seeming triviality. They tell us very little about what George Bush or his opponents would actually do as president. Yet, the lesson from the Bush presidency may very well be that in the world of image politics, no statement or political event is really trivial. Any statement, no matter how silly it may appear at the time, can play a major role in developing a president's image.

Bill Clinton: How to Reframe the President's Image?

George Bush is not the only president to have had multiple and dueling images over time. His successor in the White House, William Jefferson Clinton, has also had multiple images and serious image problems, everything from "Slick Willie" to an out-of-control womanizer. The difference is that, at various times in his run for the presidency and during his presidency, Clinton was able to craft a new image that ultimately promoted his election chances. During the 1992 presidential election, Clinton initially had a serious image problem. Many Americans thought that he had been born to wealth and privilege. In a focus group one woman summed up Clinton's image problem succinctly. When asked to pick a color to represent Bill Clinton the woman said "plaid." The message was clear to Clinton's campaign advisers. People perceived Clinton as a typical politician. This may not have been an image problem had the president-as-master-politician image still prevailed. But in the era of the Washington outsider image, this was perhaps the most deadly of all personal images. Clearly, something would have to be done to demonstrate that Clinton was not a typical politician, even if all of the evidence suggested otherwise.

To change his image his advisers placed the president in nontypical campaign settings. As the campaign heated up, Clinton appeared on MTV, played the saxophone on *The Arsenio Hall Show*, a late-night talk show, and ate at McDonalds. The strategy worked. The public began to regard Clinton in a different light. No longer was he perceived as a typical politician. Now he was seen as a new and different kind of politician, an image that certainly fit his stance as a "New Democrat" (see Goldman et al, 1994: Chapter 12).

But this new image, created for the 1992 presidential campaign, ultimately proved unsuitable for a governing president. While Clinton succeeded in getting most of his major legislative initiatives through Congress in 1993 and 1994 (with the obvious exception of health care reform), the polls indicated that few people gave him credit for reducing the deficit or for putting more police officers on the streets. Instead, the polls showed that many Americans did not perceive Clinton as being strong enough to be president of the United States. Simply stated, Clinton was not seen as being presidential, even though the polls showed that most people believed he meant well, and even that he shared their views and values.

Particularly devastating for Clinton was a trivial incident that occurred at the Los Angeles airport. Clinton was accused of holding up air traffic while he had his hair cut on Air Force One. While the press' coverage of the story later proved to be inaccurate, the White House was left with a public relations nightmare. Clinton's polls plummeted into the 30 percent range and pundits declared that his presidency was over. The haircut incident, like Bush's visit to the grocers convention, may have been a silly event hardly worth reporting. Yet, it damaged Clinton's credibility and his image. The task for Bill Clinton, then, was to once again remake his image.

After the disastrous 1994 midterm elections, in which the Republicans regained control of both the House and the Senate for the first time in 40 years, Clinton's presidency was at an all-time low. He now turned to political consultant Dick Morris, who urged the president to adopt yet another new image. He wanted Clinton to become more of a father figure for the American people; "it's time to be almost the nation's father, to speak as the father of the country, not as a peer and certainly not as a child." To accomplish this objective, Morris recommended that Clinton "stress family issues: the enforcement of child-support payments, the establishment of violence ratings for TV, improvements in education. These [issues] fit the image of a father concerned about America's children in a time when two-career families were stretched to the breaking point, growing fearful that their children were beyond their control" (Morris 1997: 181). Clinton thus adopted a substantive policy agenda, but one primarily designed to create and then advance a desired presidential image. If this new image was successful, it would catapult him into the White House for a second term as president, much as a newly tailored image had helped him win the presidency in 1992.

The development of the image-is-everything presidency is not the same as symbolic politics, since images can be created if a president or a presidential candidate adopts a strong stand on an important issue, such as George Bush's "read my lips" pledge. As the nation's father figure, Bill Clinton not only adopted strong positions on family issues, he also supported welfare reform and a balanced budget. The point is not that image politics always lacks substance. Rather, the primary danger of the image-is-everything presidency is, as noted above, that it places the public relations "cart" before the policy "horse." As Dick Morris noted, "We used polling not to determine what positions he [the president] would take but to figure out which of the positions he had already taken were the most popular" (Morris 1997: 9). Morris later commented, "Others prefer images, photos, adjectives, and negatives. We believed it was through issues that the public learned who you really were" (ibid., 123). But issues, according to Morris, did not exist in a vacuum. There was a vital synergy between issues and image. Rather than a presidential stand on the issues creating a desired image, the desired image was first identified, then congruent issues were selected that best promoted the new image. Image molded and directed the political agenda, not the other way around.

Clinton's labor secretary Robert Reich provides an example of precisely how Morris went about placing the public relations cart before the policy horse. Reich notes that on a visit by Morris to the Department of Labor, Morris told him, "You have lots of good ideas. The President likes your ideas. I want them so I can test them." Reich asked, "Test them?" Morris responded, "Put them into our opinion poll. I can know within a day or two whether they work. Anything under forty percent doesn't work. Fifty percent is a possibility. Sixty or seventy, and the President may well use it" (Reich 1997: 271).

Reich (ibid., 273) went on to describe Morris's craft as "the antithesis of leadership":

Leaders focus public attention on the hardest problems even when the public would rather escape from them. Morris, by contrast, offers nothing but diversions. That's what his polls and his ads are all about. He's a packager and promoter. To the extent B [President Bill Clinton] relies on him, B will utter no word that challenges America, no thought that pricks the nation's conscience, no idea that causes us to reexamine old assumptions or grapple with issues we'd rather ignore. B will pander the suburban swing [vote], tossing them bromides until they buy him like they buy toothpaste.

What is particularly ironic about Bill Clinton is that he was originally perceived by political pundits as a "policy wonk," someone who had a keen interest in public policy and producing solutions to the nation's problems. Initially he had adopted what he thought was the appropriate strategy for getting reelected: putting together a series of substantive accomplishments and then taking them to the public as a demonstration of his leadership ability. During his first two years in office, Clinton and a Democratic Congress had enacted an anticrime bill, the Brady [hand gun] Bill, the Medical Leave Act, and the so-called Motor Voter Act, among others. During his first year, Clinton had one of the highest success rates with Congress, as reported by *Congressional Quarterly*. It is not surprising, then, that Clinton believed these substantive achievements would help to win reelection. Yet, throughout his first two years his polls were regularly in the 40 percent range. Then, as noted earlier, in the 1994 midterm elections the Democrats lost control of both the House and the Senate, losing over 50 seats in the House! On the basis of these dramatic setbacks, Clinton came to realize that substantive accomplishments alone would not mark a successful presidency. What is important is how a president's message is communicated and how it appears to the public. This was precisely the message Richard Nixon had preached to his advisers. Having a solid record of accomplishment is no substitute for being perceived as a political success. Clinton arguably had the record, but the public did not give him credit for it. Consequently, from 1995 onward, Clinton adopted Morris's strategy. While a number of important substantive accomplishments followed, each was tailored to emphasize the predesigned image of Clinton as "father figure." From now on accomplishments would have a specific purpose: to accentuate the president's image. In this manner, substance became a mere prop to support a desired personal image.

During his second term, Clinton turned his attention to selling himself to history. He decided to address issues of broad policy importance, such as binding the nation's racial and ethnic divisions. Unfortunately, he mostly chose to address these issues by using nonsubstantive pseudo-events. For example, in Clinton's remarks of October 16, 1995, at the University of Texas at Austin, which was designed to coincide with the "Million Man March" in Washington, D.C., the message from the president was clear: "We all have a stake in solving these common problems [of race and racism] together." Clinton exalted his audience, "It is therefore wrong for white Americans to do what they have done too often, simply to move further away from the problems and support policies that will only make them worse." The president then added, "Under my watch, I will do everything I can to see that as soon as possible there is only one—one America under the rule of law; one social contract committed not to winner take all, but to giving all Americans a chance to win together—one America."

The president's objective was certainly laudatory. But how did he plan on establishing this "one America"? His solutions eschewed substance and instead embraced generalities. "First," he said, "today I ask every governor, every mayor, every business leader, every church leader, every civic leader, every union steward, every student leader—most important, every citizen—. . . to take responsibility for reaching out to people of different races; for taking time to sit down and talk through this issue; to have the courage to speak honestly and frankly; and then to have the discipline to listen quietly with an open mind and an open heart. . . . The second thing we have to do is to defend and enhance real opportunity. . . . Third and perhaps most important of all, we have to give every child in this country, and every adult who still needs it, the opportunity to get a good education."

We can contrast Clinton's speech on race with those of John Kennedy and Lyndon Johnson. Those presidents, too, spoke out passionately against racism, but they most often did so with a clear proposal in mind, to lay the groundwork for a positive legislative agenda designed to ameliorate the problems of race. Such substantive accomplishments as the Civil Right Acts of 1964, the Voting Rights Act of 1965, and the Fair Housing Act of 1968 followed their speeches. In contrast, Clinton offered no tangible proposals in his address. He did not use the opportunity to initiate a new legislative agenda. He merely urged his listeners to be more accepting and open-minded. While such moral leadership emanating from the bully pulpit certainly can have a positive impact on society, the important point is that Clinton did not commit his administration to a single legislative goal. The hopeful message of Clinton's speech was not matched with any palpable proposal for change. It is as if the mere act of speaking was commensurate with action. Having denounced racism, Clinton could now move on to other subjects, leaving behind only a legacy of words and not deeds. While such speeches promoted his image as father figure, they did little to address the nation's problems. In the end, Clinton sacrificed substance for rhetoric.

The Irony of the Clinton Presidency

One of the ironies of presidential politics is that the public actually may become accustomed to a president's negative images, which may then immunize a particular president from political fallout at a future point. For example, during the 1992 campaign, questions were raised about Bill Clinton's personal ethics. After a woman named Gennifer Flowers alleged that she had had a 12-year affair with the then-governor of Arkansas, after a letter written by a 20-year-old Bill Clinton indicated that he had dodged the draft, and after Clinton himself acknowledged that he had tried marijuana (though he "did not inhale"), he developed an image as a man of questionable ethical behavior.

Likewise, shortly before the end of the presidential campaign, then-President George Bush ate breakfast at the "Waffle House" restaurant to emphasize candidate Bill Clinton's tendency to waffle on the issues. During the 1992 vice presidential debates, when Democratic vice presidential candidate Al Gore offered a vague answer to a specific question, Vice President Dan Quayle accused him of "pulling a Clinton." Once in office, Clinton was roundly criticized by the press and by his political opponents for being too quick to compromise and for waffling on the issues. No matter how resolute Clinton tried to be, the image of him as a waffler never disappeared.

Ironically, however, both of these images may have helped Clinton in the long run. In 1997, congressional Republicans held hearings into possible campaign finance abuses by President Clinton, Vice President Gore, and other top members of the Clinton administration. Gore floundered in his attempts to explain away his activities, while Clinton boldly pronounced himself in favor of campaign finance reform. In a September 13, 1997 radio address to the American public, Clinton vowed, "There is no substitute for strong, bipartisan campaign finance reform legislation passed by Congress." Clinton noted that he had "proposed such reform when I ran for President, and I have backed reform legislation every year since then." He then noted that every year since then reform had been blocked by Congress; he did not remind his listeners that for two of those years his own party, the Democrats, had controlled Congress. Nor did the president remind his listeners that though he had, in fact, supported this legislation, he had not lobbied actively on its behalf. Nor did he admit that his administration had pushed the existing campaign finance law to the breaking point in a search for loopholes. In the end, Al Gore, who had a squeaky-clean image before the hearings, watched helplessly as his approval ratings plummeted. At the same time, Clinton's ratings held steady at about 60 percent—among the highest ratings of his entire presidency to that time.

Then, in January 1998, it was alleged that Clinton had had an affair with a young White House intern named Monica Lewinsky. He also was accused of urging Ms. Lewinsky to lie under oath about the affair. The initial public reaction to the allegations was peculiar. The first week of the scandal, polls indicated that a clear majority of Americans believed that Clinton was lying when he denied the affair. Yet, in the same polls, Clinton's approval ratings remained virtually unchanged, at 61 or 62 percent. The second week of the scandal, after Clinton had delivered his 1998 State of the Union address, an ABC News poll and a CNN/*USA Today* poll measured his approval rating at 68 and 69 percent, respectively. Other polls indicated that his approval rating was in the low 70 percent range; all of these results were all-time highs for Clinton. Later in the year, when it was announced that Monica Lewinsky would testify before a grand jury that she had indeed had sexual relations with the president, 61 percent of the respondents to a CBS News/*New York Times* poll said they approved of the president's job performance. This despite the fact that two-thirds of the poll's respondents believed the president had lied. Even when it was announced that Clinton himself would testify before the grand jury, his job approval ratings remained in the 60 percent range. Why was Clinton's approval rating so unaffected by the campaign fund-raising and Monica Lewinsky scandals?

The answer appears to be that the American public already had decided that Clinton was ethically suspect (that is, he had an image as a philanderer who was also loose with the truth). As a result, the public did not hold him to a higher standard of conduct. On the other hand, in the fund-raising case, the public expected more from Al Gore. Once his image as the "Mr. Clean" of politics was questioned, his ratings went into a veritable free fall. This is an example of one of the many ironies of image politics; Clinton's negative images actually protected him from political harm's way. Had he had a more favorable public image when news of either of these scandals was first reported in the press, it is likely that he would have experienced greater political fallout from them. Clearly, then, in examining the personal images of presidents we need to be concerned with both their positive and negative effects.

Conclusions

Since Richard Nixon's presidency, when the image-is-everything presidency was established, personal images have been created and disposed of with almost reckless abandon. While images, in general, are everything, the image of the moment is nothing more than a convenience, meant to sell a candidate or an incumbent president like a box of cereal. In this process, the White House staff, and presidents themselves, have become more concerned with image creation than with the substance of public policy. In fact, in many cases, substance has taken a backseat to image making, becoming a mere prop for it.

In the next two chapters we will examine how policy substance has become less important over time. Chapter 4 examines how presidential campaigns have become less substantive in recent decades. Chapter 5 will document and examine the increased role of rhetoric in the presidency.

4

The Constant Campaign

We created the first fully advertised presidency in U.S. history.

—Dick Morris

The Clintons and Gores walk from the bus to a rally in Centralia, Washington, on September 19, 1996, on a campaign swing through the northwest. Photo courtesy Reuters/Mike Theiler/Archive Photos, reprinted with permission.

In today's presidency one of the most direct sources of image creation is the presidential campaign. Emphasis on *image* first took hold in electoral politics as early as 1968, when campaign handlers began marketing candidates as if they were products. Then, more recently, two additional things occurred. First, campaigns themselves became progressively longer, often beginning more than two years before the presidential election. Second, the tactics of image-based campaigning were adapted to the goal of creating and selling *policies* as well as candidates. The result has been that today not only is a president running for reelection almost from the beginning of his first term, but at the same time he is also campaigning for a policy agenda that promotes a desired personal image. This is what we mean by the term *constant campaign*. The characteristics of product-marketing are so pervasive in elections and in policy debates that the differences between them, and thus between governing and electioneering, have become almost indistinguishable. Selling a president becomes more important than selling his agenda—and, increasingly, he is unable to project any clearly substantive agenda. Reelection is the only goal.

As we noted in Chapter 2, for most of U.S. history, presidential candidates did not take an active role in their campaigns. For the most part the candidates relied on surrogates from their parties or other groups that supported them to campaign on their behalf. This was largely due to the public expectations of the time. Also there were practical reasons for a lack of direct involvement by candidates in presidential elections. Until the twentieth century there was no broadcast media that could instantly reach the entire country, and candidates simply did not have the available means to traverse large sections of the country in short amounts of time to make personal appearances. Campaigning thus had to be done by supporters and through newspaper accounts.

By the early part of the twentieth century, norms and public expectations began to change. Especially after the advent of radio, presidential candidates began to participate in the public part of the election process much more directly. To some degree, they also used the medium to influence public opinion during their administrations. Franklin Roosevelt in particular made skillful use of radio in the 1930s and 1940s to convey an image of intimacy and to enhance public support for his policy agenda while in office. As early as 1952, Dwight Eisenhower, who benefited from an unusually powerful and favorable image long before his run for the White House, recognized the importance of salesmanship in elections. He employed a professional advertising agency on his campaign, and they were kept on a retainer through his first term. In 1956, the national Republican chairman, Leonard Hall, who was quite open about their role, said, "You sell your candidates and your programs the way a business sells its products" (McGinniss 1970: 21).

Television created a new and unprecedented opportunity for candidates to construct a carefully honed image they could sell to voters. Richard Nixon is usually credited with being the first to make organized and methodical use of television for such a purpose, in the election of 1968. As documented by Joe McGinniss in *The Selling of the President 1968*, from its beginning the Nixon campaign was staffed by men from the world of advertising and marketing, rather than the political operatives and party functionaries who had traditionally held such positions. Nixon blamed his 1960 electoral defeat on television and the poor image it portrayed of him. In 1968 he was determined to turn the medium of television to his advantage.

The result was primary and general election campaigns that did not emphasize Nixon *the man* as he really was, but the presidential *image* that Nixon wanted to project. He and his advisers actively created and promoted the Nixon image using the marketing techniques of Madison Avenue. At the same time they did not emphasize policy differences between the candidates regarding the pressing issues of the day, or Nixon's prescriptions for dealing with national problems. By 1968 Nixon had come to believe that such an issue-oriented approach required too much attention from the average voter. He was convinced "that he lost elections because the American voter was an adolescent whom he tried to treat as an adult" (ibid., 24–25).

He therefore needed to sell himself just as a product is sold; people would cast their votes for president for the "man," that is, the image, that seemed most presidential, not because of some arcane and complex policy arguments. In fact, Nixon refused to discuss his plan for concluding the Vietnam War, maintaining that it was necessary to keep it secret, which of course denied any opportunity to debate its merits as an electoral issue. Instead, the focus was again on advertising the *image* Nixon wanted to portray: a serious-minded, stable, experienced, and dignified politician. It is largely because of the success of this strategy that the election of 1968 was a pivotal one. It demonstrated to future presidential candidates and political pundits alike that image should take preeminence over policy substance.

According to Gary Rose, the trend that began in 1968: "The careful cultivation of candidate imagery and the emergence of media consultants as principal strategists within the context of the presidential campaign organizations was institutionalized during the 1976 presidential campaign" (Rose 1997: 78). Rose continued, "[Jimmy Carter's media consultant, Gerald] Rafshoon, like all media consultants in the post-1968 era, emerged as a central campaign advisor" (ibid., 75). For example, "in one five minute campaign biography, Carter was seen walking through a peanut field in Georgia clad in blue jeans and workboots joking with Miss Lilian, his elderly mother. The image was clearly that of an honest and simple farmer; a man of the soil with great integrity" (ibid., 75).

These ads were part of an orchestrated effort to portray Carter as an honest, populist outsider. The image was skillfully packaged and it resonated with voters. The ads were not aimed at enumerating any differences in the philosophy of government or of preferences in policy between Carter and the incumbent president, Gerald Ford.

Since 1968, only the 1980 campaign between President Jimmy Carter and Ronald Reagan placed considerable emphasis on substantive policy issues or core ideological values. The other campaigns have turned on broad and purposely vague impressions of individual candidates invented and sold by increasingly sophisticated marketing teams that have little interest in anything but winning the contest. These campaigns have stressed slogans (such as Reagan's 1984 "It's morning in America" or Bill Clinton's 1996 "Help me build a bridge to the 21st century") that purposely avoided a real discussion of the issues. Little attempt was made to build a mandate for a second-term policy agenda. For a candidate to plan how he will actually govern following an election has indeed become something of an afterthought. Creating an image conducive to winning elections has become more important during the campaign than articulating a realistic agenda.

The election of 1996 continued and expanded this pattern of placing image making before substance, perhaps making it the only factor in presidential campaigning. As Dick Morris's statement at the beginning of this chapter suggests, advertising the presidency as if it were a product or a service was a successful strategy. In addition, in his 1997 book *Behind the Oval Office*, Morris, who was Clinton's chief campaign adviser, brags about his role in the 1996 campaign, in which he advanced the image-driven presidency. Morris was not a Democratic partisan or a policy advocate, but rather a free-lance campaign manager, a "hired gun" who had worked for candidates of both parties and various ideological persuasions throughout his career. Morris repeatedly describes in detail how he saw policy positions as useful or worthwhile only to the extent that they enhanced the image that he wanted to advertise for Clinton's reelection. Clinton himself is depicted as being quite comfortable with this approach. In fact, it is Clinton who solicited Morris's aid because his own policy-minded staff members were not sufficiently image-conscious. The book describes intense disagreements between the

White House staff people—for example, Harold Ickes, George Stephanopoulos, and Leon Panetta, political professionals concerned with policy issues—and Morris, whose preferences were for gearing issues toward his reelection strategy. Prior to Morris's own self-destruction (it was revealed that the married Morris had sex with a prostitute), there was no effective effort to minimize his influence over the policy process.

But the price of election or reelection via such means is a high one when it affects a president's ability to govern. Image alone does not create the types of coalitions and support from other politicians and institutions that a president needs to govern. Once in office a new president has done relatively little to prepare for the job of governing, and a second-term president may have abandoned the issues he needs to build a governing coalition. To understand how image has come to dominate substance, we need to examine campaigning in a historical perspective.

A Historical Perspective

The election process has not always been dominated by paid political consultants, polling, focus groups, and canned campaign speeches. For much of our nation's history the political parties played a major role in choosing the candidates who would represent them in the fall presidential election. On the other hand, image in some form has almost always played a central role in presidential campaigns. To demonstrate these points, and to show differences between present and past elections, an examination of the 1920 presidential election is instructive. As we noted above, today presidential candidates begin running for office well before the presidential election year. Many candidates are on the stump as much as three years prior to the election. This elongated nomination process, however, is a fairly recent development. For the 1920 election, however, delegates of the national Republican Party convened in Chicago, Illinois, on June 8, 1920. Their chief task over the next twelve days was to nominate a ticket that would then run in the national election for the presidency five months away in November. Past campaigns were thus of much shorter duration than modern ones.

The outcome of the national convention, which is now almost always decided well before the convention actually begins, was also undetermined. Who the presidential nominee would be no one, not even the party "insiders," could know. *Primary elections*, which allow voters in individual states to pick each party's candidates, and which usually decide who the nominee will be, were not common in 1920; only sixteen states had them. Besides being relatively rare, primary elections were not very important when it came to the business of selecting a party's candidates. Groups of delegates who were chosen by the party organizations in each state made those decisions at the party's national convention.

Of course the deliberations at conventions did not start completely from scratch. The presidency has always been the most prestigious office in American politics, and in 1920 three prominent figures from the Republican Party arrived at the convention substantially ahead of any others in national reputation, delegate support, and financial resources. Perhaps the most famous on the national level was General Leonard Wood. Wood was a military figure, a hero from the recently concluded First World War and former chief of staff of the Army. A second competitor, Illinois Governor Frank Lowden, also had considerable support among the convention's delegates. The governor of a large and powerful state, he was also a well-known political figure around the country. The third major contender for the nomination was Senator Hiram Johnson from California. Senator Johnson was another very well-known figure at the time. He had run for vice president eight years earlier with former-president Theodore Roosevelt on the Progressive Party ticket.

Most observers of the convention, as well as participants, expected one of these three men to be the Republican candidate in the November presidential election. After four ballots, none of the three front-runners had been able to secure the votes necessary to win. The deadlocked convention adjourned until the following day so that party leaders and delegates could reassess their options, and candidates could consider their strategies. The next day the process of voting began again. Finally, on the tenth ballot, a winner was declared: a dark horse candidate, Warren G. Harding of Ohio, would be the Republican candidate for the White House in 1920. Just nine months later, in March of 1921, he was inaugurated as the twenty-ninth president of the United States. Of course the question on the minds of nearly everyone in the country in June of 1920 was: Who was Warren G. Harding? Today, by the time candidates are nominated they are generally well-known political commodities. Even individuals such as Jimmy Carter, Michael Dukakis, and Bill Clinton, all state governors who were little known prior to their entry into the race for the nomination, were well known by the American people by the time they were officially nominated.

In contrast, in 1920 certainly anyone but a dedicated aficionado of national politics could be forgiven for knowing next to nothing about Harding. The sum of his experience in national politics was one term as a U.S. senator from Ohio. During Harding's tenure in Congress the nation had dealt with some of the greatest political issues in its history, including American involvement in the First World War; the introduction of Prohibition; the passage of a Constitutional amendment giving women the unrestricted right to vote in national elections for the first time;

and the creation of the League of Nations, forerunner of the United Nations. Yet Harding had been, if anything, conspicuously absent from leadership on any of these issues, content to vote along party lines most of the time without contributing much to the political dialogue surrounding these important matters. This was a pattern he continued for the most part throughout the presidential campaign. In fact, Harding hardly campaigned at all, remaining instead at his home in Marion, Ohio, where he spoke to groups of reporters and supporters who came to see him about almost anything but his positions on the issues of the day.

So how had Warren G. Harding become the Republican nominee for the presidency over the likes of Wood, Lowden, and Johnson, all of whom had much more substantial political credentials? Part of the answer was that the three front-runners were so identified with strong positions on the political questions of the time. Strong leadership on controversial issues tends to make the leader controversial, as well. Enthusiastic supporters of Wood, Lowden, or Johnson often had equally vehement aversions to one or both of the other two candidates, while few delegates had any animosity toward Harding. Also in his favor, Harding was personally charming and likable, strikingly handsome, and, importantly, was "presidential" in his appearance and bearing. The decision to nominate Harding had actually been made by a handful of the party's most influential leaders who had met to resolve the deadlock. One of those present was Harding's savvy campaign manager, Harry Daugherty, who convinced those assembled that Harding was the perfect compromise candidate. By the reckoning of the Republican power brokers, Harding's lack of prominence or an established national image was one of his biggest selling points. Daugherty had confidently predicted such an outcome before the convention. What Daugherty had realized was that the most important factor in the coming election would be the candidate's *image,* and that Warren Harding presented the perfect background on which to create an image that could win the White House for the Republican Party.

In this way, Harry Daugherty was most certainly ahead of his time. The challenge he was presented with after the nomination was one that would probably give a modern campaign manager many sleepless nights: Daugherty and the Republican Party's campaign machinery had just over four months to convince the American electorate that a man most of them had never even heard of should be their next president. They succeeded. On November 2, 1920, Warren G. Harding won 61 percent of the popular vote, 26 percentage points ahead of his Democratic rival James M. Cox. Harding also won the electoral votes of 37 of the 48 states.

In some respects, then, the campaign had similarities to modern campaigns. As we noted in Chapter 2 with regard to the 1840 and 1860 elections, issues were deemphasized and the candidate's image given preeminent importance. There is a major difference, however, between those campaigns and today's campaigns. In 1840, 1860, and 1920, party insiders ultimately decided who would be their party's nominee. In this way, the parties retained control over the candidates who ran for president. Today, candidates hire their own campaign teams, often distancing themselves from their own party apparatus. The national party organization and party insiders thus generally no longer have a major role in securing the nominee they most prefer. As a result, candidates such as Jimmy Carter, who was certainly not the favorite of the Democratic Party establishment in 1976, can secure their party's nomination. Hence, while Harding may have been an unknown candidate, he still served the Republican Party's political interests in 1920. The same could not be said for Carter and the Democratic Party in 1976.

The Elongated Electoral Process

The original system for the election of a president was very different from the process we employ today. A simple reading of the portion of the Constitution that enumerated the institutions and procedures for selecting the chief executive does not reveal much about those differences. Then, as now, an absolute majority of the votes in the Electoral College was the sole criterion for election to the presidency. It is necessary, however, to look beyond the constitutional provisions to gain insight into how the electoral process really works. The constitutional rules tell us virtually nothing about the selection of the candidates from whom the Electors choose. At best, the rules in fact *begin* at the end of what we know today as a very long and complex process. And with the advent of the constant campaign, the argument can be made that now the campaign process never really ends at all (for example, Clinton began campaigning for reelection from his first day in office).

In the beginning, presidential elections were relatively elitist affairs with little popular input. As such they could be conducted fairly quickly and with little of the time-consuming efforts necessitated by campaigns aimed at large portions of the public. Congressional caucuses nominated candidates, and state electoral delegations chose from among them. "In the first election, in 1789, the process took four months from beginning to end: Electors were chosen the first Wednesday in January, they met in the states to vote the first Wednesday in February, and the votes were counted on April 6. In 1792 the second election took even less time" (Thomas, Pika, and Watson 1994: 44).

Today, the presidential campaign is a process that can be divided into three chronological phases: pre-primary activities, the primary elections, and the general election campaign. Rather than looking at these phases separately, how-ever, it is also informative to examine the factors inherent throughout the process that have contributed both to its total lengthening and to its domination by im-ages instead of substantive concerns.

Three factors of change in recent times have conspired to lengthen presiden-tial campaigns and rob them of substantive implications. First was reform of the nominating process brought on by the rise of direct primaries, which in the last thirty years has reduced the influence of party leaders and put more power in the hands of rank-and-file members (Thomas, Pika, and Watson 1994: 48). Second, the campaign finance reforms of the 1970s hugely increased the role of fund-raising in campaigns, forcing candidates to begin the drive to raise money well in advance of primary elections in order to even enter the race with any hope of victory. The third factor that has led to longer and more image-dominated cam-paigns is the decline of party loyalties among voters; this has forced aspiring can-didates to be self-sufficient in building the organization for a presidential race. This in turn requires more fund-raising and, therefore, more time. In each chronological phase of the campaign—pre-primary, primaries, and the general election—these three factors interact.

Image as a Prerequisite to Run: Pre-Primary

Presidential hopefuls spend considerable time before January of the election year laying the groundwork for their effort. This phase of the campaign process is the most difficult to define precisely in terms of dates. Groundwork for a presidential bid is often laid years in advance; some would even say that ambitious men (and probably women) have spent the better part of their lives preparing for a chance to run for president. While this is undoubtedly true, the process certainly begins with the first exploratory ventures into the realm of presidential races a year or more before the first primary.

Although this period of the process often takes place "below the radar screen" of the general public's awareness, it can be of vital importance to a would-be can-didate's prospects. This phase is the first opportunity to begin promoting an im-age that is conducive to winning in the long term, and hopefuls cannot afford to waste it. The campaigning in this phase is often not primarily directed at the pub-lic, but at important contributors and party leaders. For this reason it has been described as the *invisible primary* (Buchanan 1995: 237). With its lack of a lot of public attention, this phase is the most similar to the "smoke-filled room" sce-nario of 1920. A prospective candidate must convince the elites who control needed financial and political resources that he or she is a viable candidate. This is necessary to make a primary campaign even possible. As one writer put it, "The vetting begins during the 'invisible primary' period, often a year or more before the first electoral test. In reality, some apparently well-qualified candidates are eliminated for lack of money or supportive media coverage. The nominating process is a multistep endurance test for candidates" (Buchanan 1995: 237).

It is somewhat ironic that it is during this period of relatively low public attention that a prospective candidate is most likely to advocate specific, even controversial issue positions. One reason for being specific, even controversial, is to gain some attention from the media early in the process. Candidates can begin to get some recognition, but enough time remains for them to modify positions in a way that enhances their later chances. Ideas or aspects of images that fail to resonate with targeted groups can still be dropped or modified, while other positions can be adopted or emphasized. A second reason for emphasis on issues at this time is that in this, the least-scrutinized, phase of the process, aspirants must raise enough money to be viable in the primaries. The relatively small but active and powerful groups and wealthy benefactors candidates must appeal to at this point are likely to have a more narrow and well-defined agenda than is true of voters generally. (We talk more about the role of funding in a following section, but the fact is that fund-raising and image-building in the pre-primary phase are so interrelated in the primary process that it is impossible to completely separate the two in a discussion.)

Even potential candidates who have relatively few financial concerns see the advantages of an early start toward building a presidential image in the public's awareness. In June 1959, over a year before the 1960 Republican Convention, Nelson Rockefeller, the well-known governor of New York, began his campaign "exploration" by converting two large office buildings owned by his family in New York City into campaign staff offices. The staff included an "image division" of "top-drawer" Madison Avenue types to handle problems of personal public relations. A logistics division arranged his appearances as governor with an eye toward his possible presidential run (White 1961: 85).

Image as a Prerequisite to Run: Direct Primaries

In the early part of the nineteenth century political parties were organized, and they adopted their own internal procedures for nominating candidates, who would then be promoted for office by the parties' campaign organizations. During this same period of time, general elections themselves became much more populist affairs, and candidates (or their proxies) had to begin to campaign for support among the common people of the country. For the remainder of the nineteenth and well into the twentieth century, however, this process of selecting a party's candidates remained fairly closed to the rank-and-file supporters of the parties, let alone to the general public. The major parties' delegates, mostly selected from the party organization in each state, would then go to the party's national convention and select the party's nominees. Who the delegates to the national convention were and, more importantly, who they voted for when they got there were not determined by a popular vote. The internal workings of the parties put cliques of influential leaders who represented "the party faithful and activists—groups likely to be unrepresentative of the broad membership of either political party or of voters in general—in control [of nominations] by default" (Buchanan 1995: 229).

Therefore, as far as the average citizen was concerned, the presidential campaign began after the conventions or just a couple of months before the general election. In fact, party leaders who "controlled" the votes of groups of delegates were still the most important determiners of presidential nominations within the major political parties until the end of the 1960s. Writing about the Democratic Party's national convention in 1960, Theodore White commented, "The convention was not a free and popular vote, but would be controlled by groups that were more influential in the convention than they were in the country as a whole. Kennedy had to go into the primaries, not through the backroom negotiated nomination process" (White 1961: 69).

The primaries that Theodore White refers to were also different from the familiar pre-convention contests of today. In 1960 they still were not common. There were, "in all[,] 16 states that engaged in primaries in 1960, and not all could be entered by a given candidate for fear of offending a favorite son" (ibid., 70). White shows that in 1960 the nomination process was only beginning to change. John Kennedy was able to demand serious consideration at the convention because he had done well in the primaries leading up to it, but the final decision regarding the party's presidential candidate still rested with a small group of leaders. It was not until the 1970s that direct primary elections in which ordinary rank-and-file voters within the parties cast ballots for the person they wanted to be the party's nominee[1] became such an important factor in choosing a party's ticket. As of the 1996 election, 39 states conduct direct primaries to choose their delegations to the national conventions. It would not be accurate to say that primaries closely reflect the preferences of the general electorate. Primary voters tend to be much more ideologically oriented and politically active than the average person. Still, the overall effect of direct primaries has been to broaden the base from which to select candidates beyond the choices of a handful of party leaders. This in turn has weakened the role of party leaders in the selection process, encouraging candidates to run as Washington outsiders. It has also reduced the influences of these party officials over the policy agenda that individual candidates adopt. While in the past the election season developed an agenda, today agenda development is left to individual candidates. And while in the past the election season could be used to construct a presidential image for a candidate, today that image has to be developed before an aspirant can realistically expect to even begin a primary campaign.

Although a small group of party leaders no longer determine candidacies, it would be an exaggeration to say that nominations are now entirely populist decisions. One result of the rise of primaries is that nominations are now heavily influenced by activists who are dedicated to what is often a small part of the party's agenda, and who are concerned more about their specific policy interests than about the party's broader goals. The rise of direct primaries has made party nominations more democratic affairs than they were in the past, but who will head a party's ticket in the general election is still not entirely determined by who the party's rank-and-file supporters would necessarily prefer. But at the same time, the need to appeal to large numbers of voters even to win a party's nomination has made candidates more reliant upon constructed images, and from a much earlier point in the process than was true in the past. It has also greatly lengthened the electoral campaign process, probably inevitably. Today, even after the pre-primary selection phase, a candidate for the White House must in fact be able to run two successive national campaigns: a primary campaign among the voters of his or her party to secure its nomination, followed, the candidate hopes, by the general election campaign to win the office of president. So while in 1920 Warren G. Harding could begin at the end of June to campaign for the office he would win on November 2, today candidates launch campaigns up to four years before the election, spending millions of dollars in pursuit of the office.

Precisely when the pre-primary phase gives way to the primary campaign phase is difficult to pinpoint. The two certainly overlap; candidates must continue to court elite support throughout the primaries, and they often begin their direct appeals to the parties' voters long before officially declaring their candidacy for the nomination. George Bush, for example, practically moved to Iowa nearly a year before that state's caucus in order to actively campaign among Republicans for the party's nomination in 1980. The most unambiguous indicator that a primary campaign has begun is probably when a candidate "officially" announces that he or she is a candidate and qualifies to have his or her name on a state party's primary ballot.

The primaries are of course not a single election (though multiple states often hold their primaries or caucuses on the same date), but rather a moving series of elections that lasts for a grueling four months (though this process may be short-ened somewhat in 2000 by the introduction of a new western states Super Tues-day primary election day), with candidates criss-crossing the entire country in the process. In all, 39 states held direct primary elections in 1996. New Hampshire traditionally hosts the first primary in the country in February, and any candidate who hopes to win a nomination will have spent a tremendous amount of time campaigning in the small state during the weeks and months before that.

As political scientist Austin Ranney has said, the nominating portion of the campaign is more important than the electoral stage, because "the parties' nomi-nating processes eliminate far more presidential possibilities than do the voters' electing processes" (quoted in Thomas, Pika, and Watson 1988: 59). Because the primary contests are serial in nature, later elections are inevitably influenced by those that went before, making early elections especially critical for nomination candidates. In the 1980 primary cycle, for example, two states with less than 3 per-cent of the nation's population, New Hampshire and Iowa, received 31 percent of the media coverage accorded the primaries, while the 46 states with 79 percent of the population got less than half of the media coverage (Adams 1987: 45). In or-der to continue, a nomination-candidate must appear to be a winner as early in the cycle as possible. Poor performance in a couple of early primaries almost guarantees that a candidate will not make it to the party convention—the mo-mentum of primary campaigns usually dictates that early winners gain support and resources. This makes it even more important for candidates to amass as much money as they can in the pre-primary phase. Only a large funding-reserve can immunize a candidate for nomination against early defeats, and then not for long. In 1992 Paul Tsongas was able to win the greatest number of primary dele-gates in the New Hampshire Democratic primary, but his campaign soon ran out of money and he was forced to abandon his bid. Bill Clinton, on the other hand, went into the 1992 primaries with the best-financed campaign among the De-mocrats, and so was able to withstand the early setback of losing (Buchanan 1995: 230). Similarly, the fact that George Bush's effort in 1988 was well financed en-abled him to survive an early loss to Bob Dole in Iowa.

In the primary elections, fund-raising and voter appeals are necessarily inter-twined: More money means more contests can be entered, while more votes means more money can be raised for elections later in the cycle. The importance of early contests, however, has become even more apparent in recent times, as the primary elections have become "front-loaded"—that is, concentrating big states with the largest numbers of delegates near the beginning of the season. In 1992, for example, about one-third of the Democratic Party delegates had been selected by the time the polls closed on Super Tuesday (the second Tuesday in March, on which most of the southern states and various other states around the country hold their primary elections). "This is usually enough to identify a clear front-runner with sufficient momentum to draw media attention and money away from the other candidates" (Buchanan 1995: 226).

A candidate can never forget that delegates are what the primaries are ultimately about. Money needs to be translated into votes, and the primaries are the candidates' first electoral tests. In the end, a candidate must win the votes of a legion of individuals, the vast majority of whom will never contribute a dime to a campaign coffer. Primaries are crucial because they are the candidates' first chance to convince others that they have "what it takes" to be president—a presidential image. "Survey data also allow us to examine how voters perceive the images of presidential candidates in elections such as those of 1980 and 1984. Research indicates that candidate image is a critical component of voters' decisions (Rusk 1987) and has two dimensions: the personal qualities voters find important in presidential candidates and the job competence they seek from candidates across a range of national problems" (King and Ragsdale 1988: 390). Here the very nature of campaigns is an important test:

> It [the perception of being qualified] is reinforced by credible performance of the public and organizational tasks required during the long campaign for the presidency. The personal qualities that are most helpful to being president can be separated into 2 types: 1) demanded by the electorate and 2) demanded by the office. 1 includes reaching and inspiring audiences, likability, morality. 2 includes coping with frustration, the expedience of deceit, high workload, constant flattery. (Buchanan 1995: 236- 237)

The sheer stamina needed to persevere through the tortuous length of a primary season has come to be seen as a telling test of mettle in and of itself. The ability to withstand its rigors can itself be image-enhancing. When a candidate forgoes the process purposely, as did independent candidate Ross Perot in 1992, he denies himself the chance to show the public that he has at least part of what is needed to be president:

> By operating outside this moderating machinery in 1992, Perot evaded the revealing test of mettle that is imposed by the traditional rigors of primary campaigning. . . . Thus, a major concern about the Perot-style independent candidates is their sidestepping of the rigors of the primary process. Surely one [reason for his drop in the polls] was his reluctance to hang in when the going got tough. (Buchanan 1995: 231–239)

The ability to meet the rigorous demands of the election trail were emphasized by Ronald Reagan in 1980 and 1984 and by Bob Dole in 1996. Both candidates felt compelled to address the perception of some in the country that they were too old for the presidency. Dole took this image-building challenge to a dramatic extreme by engaging in a marathon of sleeplessness at the end of the campaign. The intended implication was that anyone who could demonstrate such stamina when needed possessed the fortitude to be president, regardless of his age.

During this long campaign period, as hopefuls try to appear more presidential than their opponents, the demands of image-building and campaigning mean there is less time for actual governance. An entire year is now taken up with presidential campaigning, and neither the president nor Congress can ignore the extended election period. In addition, the attention of the nation begins to turn to the upcoming presidential election after the midterm elections, with the press speculating on which candidates will enter the race and with candidates forming Exploratory Committees to determine if their candidacies would be viable. In addition, fund-raising and early campaign appearances in states such as Iowa and New Hampshire are common. Hence, almost two years of the four-year presidential term are now overcome with presidential politics. When one subtracts the months prior to the midterm elections, when House and Senate seats are chosen, the president today has less than 2 years in which to govern without a constant reference to elections.

Image in the End

Closing the Deal

The final phase of the presidential campaign epic is the campaign between the parties' tickets, which culminates in (the formality of the Electoral College, under normal circumstances, notwithstanding) the election on the first Tuesday after the first Monday in November. "Traditionally the general election campaign begins on Labor Day and runs to election day . . . but the planning for modern campaigns begins once the identity of the major party nominees becomes clear" (Thomas, Pika, and Watson 1994: 49–50). In other words, even before the party conventions, the front-runner for nomination has, ideally, already begun to switch gears in his campaign strategy and tactics. In many important ways, the general election is a completely different campaign from the primaries, and the transition can be treacherous. "In the general election the audience expands greatly—more than twice as many vote as in the primaries" (ibid., 67). Candidates need new strategies to win support from voters who supported other candidates in their own party primaries, and from the huge numbers of independent voters who did not participate in the primaries but whose images of the candidates were nevertheless formed in the primary campaigns. Ideally, a candidate also wants "crossover" support from voters who typically identify with the other party. Conservative Democrats, for example, were important to Ronald Reagan's victories in 1980 and in 1984, particularly in southern states.

Because the primaries are such an important source for voters in regard to a candidate's image, candidates often experience unique and difficult problems in the general campaign. For most of the year preceding the general election, the candidates now facing each other ran against members of their own party and appealed to constituencies in that party alone. Now that he or she has been nominated, the new candidate must begin projecting an even more widely appealing presidential image, which often means trying to *undo* the damage that the primary races caused to their images and to the unity of their parties. Because primaries are now so important in presidential elections, they are in many ways more hard-fought and bitter than general elections.

Observers of intraparty primaries in these days of reduced party influence are familiar with the phenomenon of the primary "bloodbath," in which hopefuls of the same party engage in "fratricide" and leave each others' images so badly damaged that the eventual candidate is doomed to lose the general election. This can also happen in presidential races. An excellent example of this occurred during the 1980 Republican primaries. Over several months, nomination-candidate George Bush assailed Ronald Reagan's proposed economic policies as "voodoo economics," a term that resounded in the media. When the Republican convention then produced Reagan at the top of its ticket, with Bush as his running mate, Bush was put in the unenviable position of having to explain, in much less time, why he now favored the same policies he had derided in the primaries. Of course, the Reagan-Bush ticket bested the incumbents Carter and Mondale by a very comfortable margin in the November election. But the image of George Bush as a vacillator who did not have strong or genuine convictions would resurface to vex him later (see Chapter 3).

Another example of the dangers inherent in the conflicting demands of primary and general campaigns can be seen in what happened to the Democratic ticket the same year. The incumbent, President Carter, was challenged for the party's nomination by Senator Edward Kennedy. Carter and his staff were determined not simply to win the nomination, but to use the process for image-building as well. They became so preoccupied with winning the party's primaries by a margin that showed how strong the president's support in the country was, compared to Kennedy's, that the Carter campaign was left poorly prepared to address the "real" challenge of Ronald Reagan in the general election.[2]

The mere two or three months between nominating convention and election day leaves very little time to get across a coherent message, let alone change or modify an image that has developed over a much longer period. The irony is that while presidential campaigns as a total process have become, in reality, inordinately long, the actual formal competition between the party tickets is as brief as ever. The brevity of the general election campaign also makes it a period of intense spending. Because the candidates in the general election must reach more voters and in a much shorter time than in the primaries, most money is spent on the mass media. Since 1952, television has been the chief source of campaign information for most Americans. In 1988, television ads accounted for 68 percent and 51 percent, respectively, of what the Bush and the Dukakis campaigns spent between the primaries and the election (Thomas, Pika, and Watson 1994: 74).

Image to Raise Money, Money to Build Image: Fund-Raising

As campaigns have gotten longer, and primaries have become more important, money has also become much more crucial to the election process. Of all the problems inherent to modern campaigns the role of money is perhaps the most obvious. While the most commonly discussed aspect of the influence of money on politics is its implications in regard to the policy-making process, it also has tremendous consequences in that it affects the length and quality of presidential campaigns. The increased length has, unsurprisingly, made them more expensive, which in turn forces candidates to begin campaigning ever earlier in order to raise funds. A vicious cycle is thus created: A presidential hopeful must start campaigning earlier, so he or she can raise more money, so that he or she can campaign longer. Again, this leaves less time for governance, because the president is constantly traveling the country raising funds for his reelection and for other candidates of his party. Hence, along with the usual presidential duties, or hats as Rossiter (1960) called them (for example, the president as Commander-in-Chief, Chief Executive, Chief Diplomat), the president has now become the Chief Campaign Fund-Raiser. In this capacity the presidency is likely to be seen as more partisan, and individual presidents are likely to become embroiled in legal questions regarding the propriety of their actions. For example, in the case of President Clinton and Vice President Gore in the 1996 presidential campaign, questions arose as to whether campaign funds were solicited from China in return for more favorable foreign policy decisions. In addition, the numerous campaign events and the resulting congressional investigations seriously reduced the time Clinton had available to govern.

Participation in these campaign fund-raisers also requires presidents to address more specialized and more politicized audiences (see Chapter 5). As discussed above, candidates may identify with strong issue-based positions before the primary campaigns. But, if they refuse to abandon those positions if they do not pay off in terms of money, the candidates do not usually last long in the primary rounds, if they make it there at all. Exactly what a candidate must do to raise money and how early he needs to begin depends largely on the position he is starting from. As already stated, in the pre-primary phase, money is primarily at stake, money that will be used to campaign for votes later. A contender who is relatively unknown to the public, who has little or no record or image in place ahead of time, needs extra time to cultivate enough support (i.e., money) to make it to the primaries. Hopefuls who are unknown on a national level must start even earlier to try to make themselves known to voters in different parts of the country and to qualify for party ballots in enough states to be competitive in the nationwide vote. Jimmy Carter, for example, began "running" early in 1974, more than two years before the 1976 convention, at which he received the Democratic nomination for president. Carter's only political experience until then was in a relatively small state, first as a member of the state legislature and then as a one-term governor. He was well aware that in order to have a chance in 1976 against many nationally prominent competitors he had to start early to make himself familiar and appealing to the primary voters. The 1976 campaign is recounted in a book by Jules Witcover appropriately titled *Marathon* (1977). In it Witcover traces the beginnings of the 1976 Democratic presidential campaign directly back to the party's 1972 convention!

Prospective candidates who are already well known ahead of time still must start their campaigns to raise money well in advance of the first formal contests. The more money a candidate has at the beginning of the primaries, the longer the candidate can last, and in turn, the more votes he or she can accumulate. Richard Nixon, who had already served two terms as vice president and had run for president in 1960, spent most of the period between 1962 (when he unsuccessfully ran for the governorship of California) and the 1968 Republican primaries establishing a modified image—the "new Nixon"—that convinced contributors and party leaders that he could indeed be a strong presidential contender in 1968.

For incumbent presidents seeking a second term, the price tag of elections may be even higher. The president must spend time campaigning and raising huge sums of money, while at the same time still performing his duties as chief executive. As already noted, the consequences to governance of this perpetual campaigning can be severe. Much has been made of the amount of time President Clinton devoted to fund-raising activities during the 1996 campaign. Dick Morris, in his book about that campaign, makes this point emphatically. To raise massive amounts of money Clinton had to attend fund-raisers, usually outside Washington. "The president went through this agony night after night after night. I began to see what those ads were going to cost him" (Morris 1997: 150–151). From Morris's perspective, however, Clinton's efforts paid off: "No president had ever advertised even remotely this far in advance of an election and none had used issue-advocacy ads. . . . Ten million dollars was about equal to what most candidates spend on ads for the entire primary season . . . yet here we were spending it on issue ads more than a year before the election year even began" (ibid., 150). Since we are arguing that image rather than issues dominated the 1996 campaign, we would not agree with Morris's definition of "issue-advocacy ads," but regardless of what the money ultimately was used to promote—an image or issues—its raising undoubtedly required tremendous expenditures of time and energy from the president.

The Climbing Toll of Image-Building: Time and Money

The necessity of mass media advertising has probably contributed most to the total campaign cost. Television advertisements in particular are extremely costly but absolutely necessary tools for creating images appropriate to candidates' aspirations. At the same time that more money than ever before has become necessary to campaign effectively, the rules governing the way candidates can go about raising money today has made it in many ways more difficult to do so now than in the past. The broad reform of campaign financing laws that went into effect in the 1970s was a result of the Watergate scandal. Under the new laws, which were meant to curb the amount of influence large contributors had on campaigns, contributions from both individual donors and Political Action Committees (PACs) to the campaigns of individual candidates were limited. So, while elections are no longer entirely financed by a few extremely wealthy patrons or corporations or other organizations, as was true at the beginning of the century, candidates must raise smaller amounts of cash from many more sources. Again, this makes the process of fund-raising, which is already indistinguishable from campaigning, a much more drawn-out affair.

Another, very practical reason makes it more important than ever before for candidates to begin raising funds early: to allow them to qualify for federal matching funds. Presidential races are the only elections for which public funding is allocated. The money in that fund is derived from taxpayers who check off the box on their federal income tax returns that asks if he or she wants three dollars to go to the presidential campaign fund. The rules for acquiring financial help from the public coffers do not favor latecomers. To have access to these funds, a candidate must raise $100,000 in individual contributions, with at least $5,000 collected in each of 20 different states (Thomas, Pika, and Watson 1994: 59).

Images over Agendas: The Declining Role of Parties

A third factor that has changed the nature of presidential races is the decline of the power of political parties in America. The rise of direct primaries, as already noted above, is one reason why traditional party leaders have lost much of their customary influence over the nomination process. Another important reason parties have lost power over the election process is a marked decline in party loyalty among American voters. In the election of 1920, less than 5 percent of the congressional districts in the country "split their tickets"—that is, voted for a representative and a presidential candidate of different parties. In 1984, more than 40 percent of the country's congressional districts returned split-ticket results. Also in that year, 75 percent of the districts that elected Democratic representatives, many by comfortable margins, also voted for a Republican president, Ronald Reagan (Rose 1988: 122). Today, less than one-sixth of the electorate shows consistent party identification from one election to the next (ibid., 121). The fact that American voters no longer show the loyalty to political parties that they once did means that each candidate must campaign more widely and with greater personal, rather than political party, financing. As Gary Rose put it: "As the long-term influence of party affiliation has become less significant in determining voting behavior, short-term influences such as the images of the candidates and campaign issues become increasingly important with regard to structuring the vote" (1997: 64). Today, if the candidate has successfully navigated the expensive primary elections in which the voters of one party have been courted, he or she must now focus his or her sights on the general populace in order to actually win the White House. With such a large portion of American voters considering themselves independent of party labels, no candidate can hope to win the election by appealing only to those voters who identify with the party that nominated him or her. Weakening party loyalties also mean candidates must target directly many groups that used to be reliable partisan constituencies (Thomas, Pika, and Watson 1994: 77). And new groups are emerging that must be courted (ibid.). Many of these interest groups purposely hold themselves aloof from direct partisan involvement in order to better press their agenda on candidates who need widespread support in the general election, knowing that parties alone cannot provide the necessary support.

The need for campaigning does not end once a president is elected; in some ways it increases, due to the lack of a solid partisan base of support. According to journalist Sidney Blumenthal, "Once elected, candidates have to deal with shaky coalitions . . . not stable party structures. They then must try to govern through permanent campaigns" (in Kernell 1985: 138).

The lack of powerful parties in the electoral process also forces the individual candidate's organization to raise the vast amounts of money needed. A few wealthy benefactors can no longer finance a party, and through the party, the candidate of their choice. As the candidates are less beholden to the parties for money and organizational support, the parties conversely have little power over the candidates' campaigns. Today it is the candidate who adopts the party, not the other way around.

As candidates focus on their personal images, the issue-agendas that concern parties are all but totally lost in the campaign process. No candidate is going to champion, just to placate the party, a position that will cost him the nomination or the election. There is simply no incentive to do so in an era when party support is so much less important than the individual's image. Richard Nixon realized this in 1968, running his campaign greatly independent from the Republican Party organization. Bill Clinton was keenly aware of the value of separating himself from the Democratic Party, both in 1992 when he ran as a "New Democrat"—underlining his independence of party orthodoxies that he felt would hurt his candidacy—and again in 1996 when he adopted Dick Morris's "triangulation" strategy, which was geared toward emphasizing his differences with the Democratic leadership in Congress.

Who Cares?

The result of all of this is that while campaigns are perhaps more democratic in a populist sense, they are certainly longer and more costly than at any time in the country's history, and fewer citizens participate in or express any interest in elections. Since 1960, voter participation in presidential races has declined in a fairly steady fashion. In the end, the person who would be president today must campaign longer and raise more money from more varied sources than ever before. Simultaneously he must appeal to and mobilize a more apathetic citizenry than in the past. It is not difficult to see then how a candidate might come to regard quickly conveyed impressions that create a favorable image as a more effective tool for reaching those voters than the laborious and expensive process of addressing problems and issues in a more substantial way. As far as the public is concerned, when it comes to campaigning, more is definitely not better.

The public the image-sellers are targeting pays less attention to and professes to have less interest in elections than ever before. Even when voters have policy preferences, identifying a candidate to represent them is difficult. A poll taken in 1988 showed that "half or more of the respondents matched the issue position with the correct candidate only five of twenty times" (Buchanan 1995: 233). In 1992, this was true of only nine out of twenty respondents.

Some observers maintain that what candidates offer as issue stances today are in reality simply statements of unobjectionable platitudes. The test for such devices is to examine the negation of the statement. When, for instance, a candidate says that he is in favor of access to decent health care for all Americans, what would be the opposing position? Is any candidate taking a stance *against* access to decent health care? The real issue for debate is how best to go about assuring access to health care. Debating that, however, requires delving into intricacies that don't lend themselves to quick sound bites, memorable slogans, or an image of concern and caring.

The concentration on candidates' images rather than on substantive issue positions, which are much harder and more expensive to convey through television, is almost certainly one reason for the public's indifference: A content analysis of 1,559 stories about the 1992 nomination campaign on ABC, NBC, and CBS from January 1 to the end of the Republican convention on August 21 showed that only 544 stories dealt with policy issues. In 520 stories the focus was on strategies, 473 were on campaign controversies, and 373 were on "horse race" standings—simplistic reports about who was ahead at a given moment (ibid., 234). Candidates, of course, know this, and it only makes sense for them to try to craft their own campaigns to best fit the coverage they will receive.

Incumbency

The Problem with Winning

A serious problem occurs when image is what wins the presidency: The same image that was so successful at the voting booth may be a hindrance to a new president's ability to govern. Jimmy Carter, for example, found that the image which helped him win the White House in 1976—that of an honest, down-to-earth, everyday type of man, a "typical citizen" rather than a professional politician— did not serve him well once he was in office and attempting to fill public expectations of presidential performance. Electorally appealing qualities of honesty and directness may be perceived as naïveté and inexperience when the winner needs to govern. Whether Carter was or was not naive or inept once in office is not the point we are making here; rather the same *image* that had been projected with such great success during Candidate Carter's campaign became a hindrance to President Carter's performance in office. So, "while it is true that simply winning the election is a feat in itself, the ultimate goal of a president is to have some impact" (Gant and Richardson 1993: 53). The winning candidate who does not deal effectively with the wide distance between election and governance can later count on facing many obstacles that stem directly from how the campaign was won. Once in office such a president will find he has to keep campaigning, not just for reelection, if it is his first term, but for support for his programs as well. "The nature of the modern presidential campaign, which thrives on outcomes in primary elections, public funding, media consultants, spot ads, and outsider images, does little to promote presidential leadership" (Rose 1997: 78).

Reelection

The dilemma of campaign image versus governing image can become especially challenging when an incumbent president is running for reelection: He or she has to manage to be a candidate and the country's leader at the same time. Incumbency presents both inherent advantages and difficulties for presidents.

Some of the advantages are relatively easy to see. A sitting president already has national campaign experience, as well as considerable discretion in allocating benefits selectively (Thomas, Pika, and Watson 1994: 82). In other words, a president has the ability to actually deliver some programs or policies to prospective voters and supporters that a non-incumbent candidate can only promise.

Two other advantages held by incumbent presidents are resources that directly have more to do with image. One is that a president can get media coverage much more easily (and inexpensively) than can a challenger, and can use that attention for image-building. The other is image itself—a president has the unique ability to appear "presidential"; he can use the trappings of the office to create the perception that he and the presidency are properly linked. For obvious reasons, the fact that a president repeatedly appears before the public in the presidential role is an extremely powerful tool for creating and maintaining a presidential image.

Media Access

Examples of presidential uses of media resources appear in detail in Chapter 6. Here, it is sufficient to note that presidents make routine use of media, especially television, to send messages to the public. As summed up by King and Ragsdale:

> Since Harry Truman, presidents have regularly delivered major addresses to the nation, preempting scheduled programming, on radio and television. . . . [A]ddresses to the nation delivered during prime-time, are heard by well over 50 million people. Presidents have consistently asked and received permission from the three major tele-

vision networks to preempt prime-time broadcasting when delivering a speech to the American people. (1988: 250)

Such messages can have obvious campaign value for a president, even if the speech's content is not directly related to an electoral issue.

Presidential Appearances

In addition to making speeches, presidents can stage image-creating or image-enhancing events that serve campaign purposes in addition to having other relevance. Some of these are the so-called *pseudo-events*. Some, however, are genuine events of state that can be used to electoral advantage. The most readily apparent of these is probably the state visit to another country. "Trips abroad enhance image as international leader. Incumbents can do this as a campaign move" (Thomas, Pika, and Watson 1994: 109). Richard Nixon, for example, timed his historic trips to China and the Soviet Union in part to coincide with the 1972 presidential and congressional elections. Domestic trips can have substantial effects as well, especially when the large public turnout and enthusiasm for any presidential visit that is typical in most parts of America can be depicted by White House image makers as political support for the president's policies and performance.

Does the Tail Wag the Dog?

Whenever a serving president wants to run for reelection, it is inevitable that some of the president's time and energy has to be spent campaigning for the office. We have already seen that some of the duties of the presidency have inherent campaigning value of their own, regardless of specific electoral strategies, but an incumbent running for reelection will probably need to campaign for the office directly as well. A problem may arise when demands of electioneering and of governance overlap. When reelection becomes a major, perhaps overriding, goal in itself for a president, it gets harder to distinguish an incumbent's policy efforts from reelection campaigning. The potential danger to the assumed ideal of "good government" arises when policies are advanced by a sitting president not because of their intrinsic merit or a genuine conviction that they will be beneficial, but because they play well as electoral issues. Entire policy areas, such as regional-stabilization in foreign policy, that are important but too arcane or remote from popular concern to have campaign value, get ignored. Meanwhile, policy areas that resonate with voters can be turned into pseudo-events, such as a

"dialogue on racism," that showcase dramatic posturing but produce little substantive action.

Of course blame for confusing campaigning and governing cannot be placed
solely on the shoulders of first-term presidents who aspire to a second term.
While in the past it was considered inappropriate and unseemly (that is, *unpresi-
dential*) for a president to campaign for himself, a president who wants to be retained in office today cannot afford such a haughty attitude. Recent presidents
have tried to keep a difficult balance: actively seeking voter support—which the
modern public unquestionably demands they do—while trying to maintain the
dignity of the office and at least appear to exercise leadership that transcends electoral pandering. It also must be remembered that presidents "campaign" not only
for reelection to office, but also for public support for their programs and policy
initiatives. Positive public opinion, by itself, can also be among a president's most
powerful resources when trying to meet policy goals. A lesson in the consequences of keeping reelection and governing goals too separated is provided by
George Bush's unsuccessful 1992 reelection bid. As documented by Richard Waterman (1996), President Bush, who disliked campaigning, steadfastly insisted
that his White House staff and his campaign organization remain entirely separate and compartmentalized, with government business the president's priority.
In the end a president who appeared unbeatable one year before the election was
defeated after a steady and precipitous decline in popularity.

The Clinton presidency stands in stark contrast to Bush's in the realm of campaigning. Unlike President Bush, Bill Clinton has always been an avid campaigner.
His emphasis on public, campaign-style events has certainly helped him to build
public support for his programs at times, and to rehabilitate his personal image
when it has come under assault. But, it has also led to considerable criticism that
with the Clinton administration has come a new level of confusion in the roles of
governing and of campaigning. According to the critics, President Clinton never
stopped campaigning for office and failed to enter the governing mode. While it is
difficult to limit such criticisms to one president without being disingenuous, it is
true that the Clinton White House is the first to explicitly embrace the concept of
the "permanent campaign" as it has been defined by President Clinton's 1996 reelection campaign adviser, Dick Morris. According to Morris, policies should be
pushed according to the electoral value they have in a campaign. He maintains
that while it would not be desirable for a president to take positions merely for
their vote appeal, it is advisable for him to highlight the policy areas that show
him to his best advantage electorally; the importance of the policy area emphasized is secondary. As he quotes President Clinton: "Clinton probed, 'So you use
the issues you care about to show your personality. If you want to clean up nurs-

ing homes that suggests you must be compassionate. If you are for schools, you might be a person who likes kids'" (Morris 1997: 47). Morris also offers his own take on the formation of policy initiatives for their electoral value:

> I [Morris] suggested cracking down on militias. We could require that weapons inventories be filed with local police, that notice of maneuvers and training be given to local police and the FBI, and that the president alert innocent citizens by publishing a list of organizations dedicated to domestic terror. This plan was killed by adverse reaction from the Justice Department, citing civil liberties. (ibid., 123)

What we are saying is important to note about Morris's account is not whether "cracking down on militias" is or is not a desirable or a legitimate policy, but that the policy was being advocated because of its perceived electoral appeal. Whether or not such policies would actually serve any public interest is portrayed as being of little, if any, concern. This is an example of what some observers of contemporary politics have called "the tail wagging the dog"—winning elections, that is, campaigning, taking precedence over accomplishment, or image over substance. If indeed such a state of affairs has come to pass, the tool that has made it possible is the public opinion poll.

Opinion Polling

At least since the time of Franklin D. Roosevelt, presidents and presidential candidates have increasingly made use of public opinion data. Some prominent polling organizations—for example, Harris Polls—got their start this way. Candidates craft their images and strategies based on these polls. Presidents "sensitize themselves to public views by paying close attention to the results of public opinion polls. Starting with Franklin Roosevelt, presidents have hired their own pollsters" (Thomas, Pika, and Watson 1994: 111).

These data are used not only during elections, but also when presidents are trying to sell their policy goals. As in the case of campaigning, criticism of polling is not based on the idea that it is inappropriate for a president to stay abreast of public opinion. The problem arises, the critics say, when presidents use public opinion information to determine what policies and programs to devise and endorse. At worst, the president could use polling simply to pander to public perceptions instead of exercising the leadership or guidance traditionally expected from a chief executive.

The use of polling data was originally pioneered by the advertising industry. But, by 1960, presidential scholar Richard Neustadt had observed that polls by the

Gallup Organization that had been conducted monthly or bimonthly since Franklin Roosevelt's third term (1941–1945) had become "a general measure of the president's personal prestige" (Neustadt 1960).

The question, familiar to most people who pay any attention to presidential politics, was and still is, "Do you approve or disapprove of the way [the incumbent] is handling his job as president?" Further research has shown that Gallup's regular measures of presidents' "public approval" influences presidential election results, presidents' public appearances, and presidents' success with Congress (King and Ragsdale 1988: 278).

Louis Harris, founder of Harris Polls, one of the biggest national opinion surveying firms, was part of the Kennedy inner circle in Kennedy's campaign and afterward. "A student of 'depth tides' in American thinking . . . upon his description of the profile of the country's thinking and prejudices, as he found them were to turn many of John F. Kennedy's major decisions" (White 1961: 66). After the televised presidential campaign debate between Richard Nixon and John Kennedy in 1960, polling data dramatically demonstrated the impact on public perceptions of image over issues positions. By the late 1980s, the Bush administration was being regularly criticized for being driven by public opinion data, from which critics inferred that Bush lacked any real convictions, or core values, beyond telling the public things it wanted to hear. In the estimation of many, this problem, real or perceived, will continue to become more pronounced in the future.

As valuable as pollsters proved themselves to be in elections, they have also come to be prominent and influential members of White House staffs. Inevitably, the central role that polling has come to play in policy making has further blurred the line between campaigning and governing. Again Dick Morris, chief architect of Bill Clinton's 1996 reelection campaign, provides insight on how powerful opinion polling has become. Referring to his attempts to convince the president that there was no "deep sense of pessimism" running through the American public, Morris states: "When Clinton says something that basic and important, there is only one way to try to change his mind: with polling data" (Morris 1997: 188). Morris then goes on to explain how the long-term use of ads and "opinion-polling" on their effects was, at least in his assessment, the central tool in the president's reelection strategy. In Morris's opinion, "It was our ads more than anything else that created and held our lead" (ibid., 140). Of course, the real debate is not about the importance of ads, which after all can be used to promote substantial issues and elevate the quality of public debate, but the *content* of those ads. When the intended effect of advertising is simply to win an election, nothing more, then an image is more effective than a message or a plan of action. But without a message or a plan, governing becomes a much more difficult process.

Immense resources and sophistication in creating images have produced tremendous success for presidential candidates who know how and are willing to use them. For better or worse, the constant campaign, perpetually tested by opinion polls, has become a fixture in politics of the presidency. Perhaps the final assessment of the constant campaign is best expressed by presidential scholar Richard Rose: "There is a cost in perpetual campaigning. The more time spent thinking about campaign style, the less time there is to think about the substance of government. Perpetual campaigning can become an end in itself rather than a means to an end of going to Washington" (1988: 117).

Notes

1. In most cases when primary voters go to the polls on primary election day, they do not vote for a candidate, but for delegates who are pledged to support the candidate at the party's convention. Similarly, when a voter casts his or her vote for a ticket in the general election for president and vice president, the voter is really voting for Electors who are pledged to vote for those candidates in the Electoral College, not for those candidates directly.

2. This is not to suggest that the Carter team's emphasis on the Kennedy challenge was the chief cause of the president's defeat. Many variables, some of Carter's making and others not, converged to deliver the White House to Reagan in 1980.

5

....

Speaking More, Saying Less: The Pattern of Presidential Speechmaking

The more presidents talk, the less powerful any of their individual words become.

—Mary Stuckey (1991: 61)

President Bill Clinton addresses the nation from the White House after testifying for five hours to independent counsel Kenneth Starr's grand jury on August 17, 1998. Photo courtesy of Reuters/RTV/Archive Photos, reprinted with permission.

As we stated in Chapter 1, the pseudo-event has become an important tool of the modern presidency. Technically speaking, it is a staged event designed to promote a desired presidential image, though sometimes the term can be used to describe political fallout from actual events (for example, the media coverage and presidential response to Clinton's infamous 1993 tarmac haircut). But in precisely which manifestations can pseudo-events be discovered? In this chapter we examine one manifestation—presidential speechmaking. Speeches are not pseudo-events if they are substantive, that is, if they provide the public with useful information regarding what the president actually intends to do. We will argue, however, that while presidents in recent decades have been speaking more often, they have been addressing individuals at staged events, most often ceremonial and political events. Even if presidents are speaking substantively at these events, they are doing so to small, specialized audiences and not to the wider public. Furthermore, existing evidence indicates that even when presidents are addressing the nation, their speeches have become less substantive over time. Even such speeches as the State of the Union address, where presidents have generally laid out their policy agenda, are becoming pseudo-events designed to promote a president's popularity and image. Two basic causes can be identified for this reduction in substance: (1) a presidential decision, beginning with Richard Nixon, to divide presidential speechwriting from the policy-making process, and (2) the growing influence of television. In turn, as substance has declined, presidents have increasingly used speechmaking as a means of promoting their images and their popularity.

The Early Presidents

As Jeffrey Tulis wrote, "Prior to . . . [the twentieth] century, presidents preferred written communications between the branches of government to oral addresses to 'the people'" (1987: 5). In an age in which political ambition was not encouraged (see Chapter 2 of this book), presidential speechmaking was considered rather unbecoming. Largely for this reason, none of our first presidents (George Washington, John Adams, Thomas Jefferson, or James Madison) were able speakers. In fact, Jefferson was well known for his natural reticence and his inability to speak publicly (see Ellis 1997).

This "deemphasis on public speaking" did not mean "that the early presidents were blind to the emotional side of politics. Even at this early stage, presidents engaged in some small degree of 'public image-making,' particularly regarding their wealth and social status." Additionally, "Revolutionary-era presidents were . . . both conscious and oriented toward the preservation of their public images" (Stuckey 1991: 15). But they did not accomplish image making through rhetorical means. As Mary Stuckey (ibid., 16) has noted, "Even though the early presidents were conscious of their public images, this does not imply that they engaged in the kind of activity associated with 'going public.' Quite the contrary, a low profile was integral to the public images of the early presidents, who were expected to be above the fray and not to engage too blatantly in the world of partisan politics."

Most of the nineteenth-century presidents continued the pattern set by the Revolutionary-era presidents. Even a great orator like Abraham Lincoln spoke as president only occasionally and not in partisan forums. As Stuckey commented, "After his nomination . . . Lincoln greatly reduced his public appearances, since he was now a sitting president endowed with the dignity of that office, not a mere presidential aspirant. He spoke little as president, and his reputation for eloquence is based almost entirely on his inaugural addresses and the Gettysburg Address" (ibid., 21).

In fact, as can be seen in Table 5.1, only eight of our pre–twentieth-century presidents spoke more than ten times on average per year. While public speaking appears to have become more acceptable as the nineteenth century came to an end, particularly among Presidents Rutherford Hayes, Benjamin Harrison, and William McKinley, few presidents used public speaking to advance their own legislative programs or policy initiatives. Indeed, Tulis (1987: 67) has indicated that only four of twenty-four nineteenth-century presidents "attempted to defend or attack a specific bill or law" in their speeches (1987: 67).

What were the consequences of this pattern of relative presidential silence? First, since presidents did not speak to the public, they could not directly rouse the passions of the people. The Founding Fathers had feared the potential presence of a demagogue in the White House. One of the tools of the demagogue was thought to be public speech. Without access to this tool, then, presidents could not appeal directly to the worst instincts of the public. Even Andrew Jackson, who claimed to be the "tribune" of the people, and was therefore accused of demagoguery by his opponents, spoke only nine times during his presidency or about 1.1 speeches per year. Second, because most contact with Congress was written rather than verbal, there was a greater propensity for actual deliberation. This meant that ideas and substance could be more easily translated from one branch

. . . .

TABLE 5.1
Presidential Speechmaking Before the Twentieth Century

President	Total Speeches	Average per Year
Washington	25	3.1
Adams, J.	6	1.5
Jefferson	3	0.4
Madison	0	0.0
Monroe	42	5.3
Adams, J. Q.	5	1.3
Jackson	9	1.1
Van Buren	27	6.8
Harrison, W. H.	0	0.0
Tyler	5	1.3
Polk	15	3.8
Taylor	22	16.9
Fillmore	20	7.4
Pierce	20	5.0
Buchanan	9	1.1
Lincoln	78	19.5
Johnson, A.	70	17.5
Grant	25	3.1
Hayes	126	31.5
Garfield	10	14.0
Arthur	40	12.1
Cleveland	51	6.4
Harrison, B.	296	74.0
McKinley	130	32.5

SOURCE: Tulis (1987: 64).

of government to another. Third, speeches, when they were given, were rarely policy oriented. As a result, presidents were rarely perceived to be the advocates of a particular bill, never mind advocates for a broader legislative program.

The "Rhetorical Presidency" and Public Expectations

As we noted in Chapter 2, by the turn of the twentieth century a new presidential image was emerging: the master politician image. This historical image depended on personal action-oriented images. One manifestation of action was an increase in presidential speechmaking. Jeffrey Tulis has argued that **"Rhetorical Presidency"** emerged at the beginning of the twentieth century. As noted above, a few of the late-nineteenth-century presidents had begun to speak more often, but Teddy Roosevelt, who assumed the presidential office in 1901, clearly accelerated this trend. More importantly, he used presidential speechmaking for a direct purpose: to promote not only his own personal image but also specific policies and legislation. Roosevelt had found that he could not merely work behind the scenes to secure congressional support for legislation that he favored. As a result, as Roosevelt explained in his autobiography, "I was forced to abandon the effort to persuade" Congress "to come my way, and then I achieved results only by appealing over the heads of the Senate and House leaders to the people, who were the masters of both of us" (1985 edition: 367). Roosevelt thus "embarked upon a series of rhetorical campaigns to secure passage of legislation to regulate the railroads" (Tulis 1987: 95). This effort proved somewhat successful, but over time serious strains developed between Roosevelt and even his Republican partisans in Congress. Still, Roosevelt had set a precedent by speaking out publicly for policy purposes. In so doing he made it easier for his successors to address the public directly about policy-related matters. He also established the pattern of promoting a presidential agenda, in this case, his Square Deal. As Tulis commented, "We now take for granted what [Theodore] Roosevelt experienced as fresh and new. As leadership through capsulization would become routine, it would become an expectation—and as an expectation it would structure as much as service presidential policy" (ibid., 96).

"Where the early presidents led through example and policy, the presidents following [Teddy] Roosevelt increasingly would rely on the arts of persuasion" (Stuckey 1991: 25). According to Richard Neustadt, "The power to persuade is the power to bargain. Status and authority yield bargaining advantages. But in a government of 'separated institutions sharing powers,' they yield to all sides. Command has limited utility; persuasion becomes give-and-take" (1980 edition: 28–29). While the persuasion that Neustadt discussed included such techniques as backroom bargaining, over time presidential persuasion has become virtually synonymous with the art of public speaking. As Theodore Roosevelt noted in his memoirs, even in the first decade of the twentieth century the president found it necessary to go over the heads of Congress directly to the American people. A new art of persuasion was being created, one that would be central to the formulation of the image of the president as master politician.

While the presidency of William Howard Taft represented a retreat from the Rhetorical Presidency and the master politician image, Woodrow Wilson enthusiastically embraced the use of presidential rhetoric. Though personally detested by

Roosevelt, Wilson "learned much about moral suasion from him" (Stuckey 1991: 25). In some cases Wilson even bested Roosevelt. For example, Wilson became the first president in over one hundred years to deliver in person the State of the Union address before Congress. When Wilson announced his intention to do so, over a dozen senators voted to adjourn the Senate in an attempt to preserve tradition, but their effort failed. Wilson addressed the Congress the next day. The reaction was immediate and positive. "Newspapers across the country carried the short speech, whereby millions of Americans also 'heard' what Wilson had said. No previous presidential speech had reached so many people" (Gelderman 1997: 7). From this point forward, all presidents would be free to speak publicly before Congress and all would personally deliver the State of the Union address. While presidential activity in the 1920s represented a return to a less active presidency, there was no retreat from the Rhetorical Presidency. In fact, the 1920s saw the first presidential use of a new technology that could bring presidents closer than ever to the American public: radio. Warren G. Harding became the first president to use the radio to address the American public. Presidents Calvin Coolidge and Herbert Hoover also used this new technology. But it was Franklin Delano Roosevelt who combined carefully crafted and skillfully delivered presidential rhetoric with radio appeals to a mass audience. As Mary Stuckey wrote, "Unlike most politicians, FDR never forgot that radio listening was done by individuals and family groups, not by hordes who filled auditoriums. Roosevelt's ability to understand the intimacy of the new mass medium gave people the feeling that he understood them as individuals" (1991: 33).

It was Franklin Roosevelt's innate sense that he was speaking directly to individuals that more than anything else transformed presidential rhetoric and the modern presidency, as well as further advanced the image of the president as a master politician. Suddenly, people turned their attention and their expectations directly toward Washington, D.C., and the president of the United States. Roosevelt began this transformation of public expectations with his first inaugural address. According to White House aide Sam Rosenman, Roosevelt's speech promoted "the renewal of the courage and hope and faith of the American people." Within a week of FDR's inaugural address "more than a million letters and telegrams were on their way to the White House, expressing faith in him and his leadership" (quoted in Goodwin 1994: 46–47). And the mail from ordinary Americans continued to flow to the White House. As Waterman wrote, "Whereas one man had been able to answer all of Hoover's mail, a staff of about fifty had to be hired to handle Franklin Roosevelt's correspondence. His mail averaged 5,000 letters per day, increasing at times to about 150,000 letters" (1993: 25). There was of course a danger in these heightened public expectations. Presidents "who were to follow Roosevelt found a world of high, often unrealistically inflated expectations of presidential potentialities" (Stuckey 1991: 35).

Style Versus Substance

Presidents encouraged increased public expectations by speaking more often. But precisely how have presidents spoken? In Table 5.2 we break down the total number of speeches delivered by each president from 1949–1985, along with a monthly average. The data reveal that presidents are clearly speaking more often. The monthly average increased with Kennedy, and with the exception of Nixon, remained at above 20 speeches per month through the end of the period covered in the table. Ford spoke most often, delivering an incredible 42.6 speeches on average per month. The data also reveal an increase in the number of televised addresses over time, and an exponential increase in televised speeches during Reagan's presidency. While the data cover only the period up through 1985, there is no indication that presidents have spoken less since Ronald Reagan left the White House. As Carol Gelderman has noted, "Bill Clinton, in his first year as president, spoke publicly three times as often as Reagan did in his first twelve months." (1997: 8).

TABLE 5.2
Frequency of Speechmaking, 1945–1985

President	Total Speeches	Monthly Average %	"N" National Addresses per Year on Radio or Television
Truman	1407	15.1	11.3
Eisenhower	925	9.6	9.6
Kennedy	771	22.0	13.3
Johnson	1636	26.8	12.9
Nixon	1035	15.2	19.8
Ford	1236	42.6	22.5
Carter	1322	27.5	23.0
Reagan	1637	27.3	52.8

SOURCE: Hart (1987: 8 and 53).

Along with an increase in the total number of speeches, presidents have appeared at public events more often, as shown in Table 5.3. John Kennedy conducted approximately 19 public activities on average per month throughout his presidency, while Johnson conducted 24 such activities on average per month. While there was a decline in the number of public activities under Nixon—a president who was not particularly comfortable in the public eye—we see that Nixon's three successors appeared in public quite often (26 appearances for Ford, 22 for Carter, and approximately 25 for Reagan).

How substantive were these public activities? Bruce Miroff has stated that Kennedy introduced the use of political spectacles to the White House. Spectacles are "a kind of symbolic event, one in which particular details stand for broader and deeper meanings. What differentiates a spectacle from other kinds of symbolic events is the centrality of character and action." Spectacles present "intriguing and often dominating characters not in static poses but through actions that establish their public identities" (1988: 272).

Spectacles certainly would fall under our definition of a pseudo-event. By their very nature, spectacles tend to be nonsubstantive political events. As Miroff continued:

TABLE 5.3
Levels of Public Activities of Presidents, 1949–1984

President	Total Activities	Yearly Average	Monthly Average
Truman[a]	520	130	10.8
Eisenhower, I	330	83	6.9
Eisenhower, II	338	85	7.0
Kennedy	658	219	18.8
Johnson[a]	1463	293	24.0
Nixon, I	634	159	13.2
Nixon, II	204	113	10.2
Ford	756	344	26.0
Carter	1047	262	22.0
Reagan, I	1194	299	24.9

[a] Truman's administration is counted from 1949 on, while Johnson covers his entire term from November 1963 through January 1969.
SOURCE: King and Ragsdale (1988: 275).

The audience watching a presidential spectacle is, the White House hopes, as impressed by gestures as by results. Indeed, the gestures are sometimes preferable to the results. Thus, a "show" of force by the president is preferable to the death and destruction that are the result of force. . . . Gestures overshadow results. They also overshadow facts. (ibid.)

Still, spectacles are not entirely divorced from facts. "Without real events, presidential spectacles would not be impressive." Still, "some of the facts that emerge in the course of an event might discredit its presentation as a spectacle. Therefore, a successful spectacle, such as Reagan's 'liberation' of Grenada, must be more powerful than any of the facts upon which it draws" (ibid., 276).

To get a sense of how many of the president's public appearances are spectacles, and how many are more substantive events, we show in Table 5.4 a breakdown of different types of public appearances. From the data in the table, it is apparent that presidents increased the number of foreign appearances they made, particularly since Gerald Ford's presidency. But the most striking finding is the increase in the number of "political" appearances since Lyndon Johnson's presidency. Clearly, then, part of what we are seeing in terms of both increased speechmaking (Table 5.2) and public appearances (Table 5.3) is related to an increasing politi-

TABLE 5.4
Presidential Speeches and Appearances: Truman Through Reagan

President	Major Speeches	Minor Speeches	News Conf.	Foreign Appear.	Public Appear.	Political Appear.
Truman*	15	39	160	39	53	88
Eisenhower, I	21	11	99	11	75	66
Eisenhower, II	20	18	94	18	43	45
Kennedy	15	30	65	30	97	49
Johnson*	23	49	132	49	244	131
Nixon, I	23	25	30	25	166	102
Nixon, II	13	22	9	22	38	11
Ford	12	77	41	77	183	409
Carter	17	82	59	82	172	234
Reagan, I	20	78	23	78	260	206

* Truman's administration is counted from 1949 on, while Johnson's entire term from November 1963 through January 1969 is covered.
SOURCE: King and Ragsdale (1988: 262–274).

cization of the presidency. As we argued in the last chapter, presidents, especially since 1968, have adopted a veritable "constant campaign" mode. Table 5.4 provides evidence for this point. The data in Table 5.5 provides additional evidence; it shows a breakdown of the number of speeches in election and non-election years. With some variation across presidencies, we see that presidential speechmaking has increased in both election and non-election years. We cannot therefore attribute the increased propensity of presidents to speak and appear in public solely to increased presidential activity in election years. Rather, the phenomena is broader, suggesting more activity and more speechmaking throughout a president's entire term of office.

Since presidents are speaking and appearing in public more often, and since many of these are at political appearances, we can ask: How substantive are their speeches? One way to determine the substance of speeches is to break them down by the type of speeches presidents have delivered. **Major speeches**, such as the State of the Union address, inaugural addresses, and economic policy speeches, reach a wider audience and thus have the greatest potential for providing substantive information to the nation. **News conferences** also provide an opportunity for the president to supply information to the public. **Minor speeches,** on the other hand, are delivered in front of specialized audiences, and there is thus less potential for substantive policy information to reach a broader audience.

If we turn our attention back to Table 5.4, we see that the number of major speeches delivered by the modern presidents (from Truman through Reagan) did

TABLE 5.5
Presidential Speaking in Non-election vs. Election Years

President	Average "N" Non-election Years	Average "N" Election Years
Truman	122.2	244.8
Eisenhower	108.0	123.3
Kennedy	236.5	298.0
Johnson	280.0	347.1
Nixon	182.3	203.3
Ford	396.0	542.1
Carter	281.5	379.5
Reagan	293.7	382.0

SOURCE: Hart (1987: 157).

not change much over time. Of those presidents who served a full term in office, Truman spoke the least, with only 15 major speeches; Carter was next with 17. On the other hand, Nixon spoke the most, with 23 major speeches. Johnson also made 23 major speeches, but his presidency extended over a five-year period. The data for Kennedy, Nixon's second term (Nixon II), and Ford represent periods of less than one full term in office. The important point here is that the difference between the president who spoke the least (Truman) and the president who spoke the most (Nixon) was only 8 speeches over a four year period. The evidence on major speeches therefore does not support the notion that presidents are actually speaking more often.

Presidents are also delivering fewer news conferences over time. Since presidents are more likely to address substantive issues in news conferences, as well as have a national audience, this is not a propitious development. The only bright spot here is that Presidents Bush and Clinton have held news conferences more frequently than their immediate predecessors: Bush 3.0 news conferences per month, for a total of 142, and Clinton 2.8 conferences per month—during his first term—or a total of 145 (Thomas, Pika, and Watson 1997: 123).

While this is an encouraging trend, it should be noted that Clinton abruptly stopped giving news conferences as the 1996 election approached, and then held far fewer news conferences during his second term in office than during his first term.

In Table 5.4, while we see no increase in the number of major speeches, and an actual decrease in the number of news conferences conducted over time, we do find considerable variation in the number of minor speeches delivered by presidents over time. In particular, from Gerald Ford's presidency onward, presidents delivered a larger number of minor speeches. To whom, then, were they speaking in these minor speeches?

The data in Table 5.6 indicate that the most common setting for all types of presidential speeches (major and minor combined) were ceremonial occasions. Over one-third of all presidential speeches occurred at ceremonies honoring some event, group, or individual. Another 15 percent occurred at political rallies. In fact, over one-half of all speeches occur in these two types of settings, in which substance was less likely to be delineated, or it was more likely to be couched in highly partisan terminology. In contrast, only just over one-quarter of all speeches occurred at "briefings," which presumably would be the most likely forum for the translation of substantive information to the public.

The Table 5.7 data also indicate that presidents were speaking more often before local audiences and the press, before special interest groups, and before invited guests than they were to the nation at large. Indeed, only 11 percent of

TABLE 5.6
Settings for Speeches

Setting	"N"	%
Ceremony	3740	37.5
Briefing	2642	26.5
Organizational meeting	1023	10.3
Political rally	1497	15.0
Miscellaneous	1066	10.7

SOURCE: Hart (1987: 229).

Washington-based speeches were designed for a national audience, and only 7.9 percent of all speeches were directed at a national audience. So, while presidents up through Reagan were speaking more frequently, relatively few of their speaking engagements occurred before a national audience. The data clearly show that even if presidents were speaking substantively, they were doing so to ever smaller and more specialized groups of people.

But even in these settings, were presidents speaking substantively? While Franklin Roosevelt made greater use of the Rhetorical Presidency than his predecessors, he did not sacrifice substance for style; that is, he "did not govern publicly except on specific occasions and with regard to specific issues" (Stuckey 1991: 31). He delivered only a limited number of ceremonial speeches. Indeed, "Roosevelt

TABLE 5.7 Location for Speeches

Audience	Washington, D.C.		National	
	"N"	%	"N"	%
Government employees	106	1.7	142	1.4
Local/press	2797	44.9	5116	51.3
National	688	11.0	783	7.9
Invited guests	1147	18.4	1556	15.6
Special interest groups	1496	24.0	2369	23.8

SOURCE: Hart: (1987: 105 and 228).

was more likely to turn a ceremonial occasion (the dedication of a dam, for example) into an occasion for the discussion of policy issues than to turn discussion of a policy issue into a ceremonial occasion." And while "Roosevelt was clearly aware of the symbolic dimension of his actions and would often explicitly discuss some action as a symbol of a point he was trying to make, the actions were policy oriented as well as symbolic" (ibid.). Unfortunately, the evidence suggests that Roosevelt's successors have been far less interested in policy substance than in promoting political symbolism.

What has been the pattern of speechmaking since Franklin Roosevelt's presidency? In an impressive content analysis of presidential speeches made since the beginning of the twentieth century, Barbara Hinckley (1990) found that our early twentieth-century presidents—from Teddy Roosevelt to Franklin Roosevelt—were more likely to include references to policy and political mandates in their inaugural and State of the Union addresses than have presidents from Harry Truman onward. Hinckley also found that presidents from Truman onward have portrayed a highly unrealistic version of our governmental system, one in which the president is portrayed as acting alone for the nation. These presidents rarely refer in their speeches to either the separation of powers or other relevant political actors, including the Congress. Instead the modern cohort of presidents have tended to invoke religious and moral platitudes, rather than policy prescriptions. Hinckley concluded that this strategy of using "the magic of symbolism to create illusion" has its costs, which "must be considered by journalists, teachers of politics, and future presidents" (1990: 38). The cost of portraying an unrealistic version of American politics in which the president alone is capable of handling the nation's problems is that first the public develops unrealistic expectations of presidential performance, and then these ultimately devolve into greater public disillusionment with the American political process.

In summary, the evidence presented thus far indicates that presidents have spoken and appeared in public more often, but that they have not said more, especially to the nation as a whole. This then is evidence that presidential speechmaking has become a prop for various pseudo-events. What may be the most troubling aspect of this development is that the American people may be confusing public speaking and public appearances with actual presidential leadership. As one of the nation's authorities on presidential rhetoric, Roderick Hart has noted, "American voters have been led to believe that if a president can speak in public he can lead in private and that he is unable to do the latter unless he can do the former" (1987: 47). Yet the irony here is that the increased attention to speechmaking actually may leave presidents with less time for the important functions of governance. Hart continued, "Since the average modern president gives more than one . . . speech during each working day, his time on the job has increasingly become rhetorical time. All of this leaves few moments for the other sorts of things we expect a president to do—namely, to think" (ibid., 197). Another irony is that the increased preponderance toward presidential speechmaking may be obfuscating the issues, rather than making them easier for the public to understand. As Hart observed:

> . . . rhetoric may now be the primary means of personal assertion, the primary means of performing the act of presidential leadership. . . . The great advantage of this political convention is that even if leaders know not which direction to take, they can still speak in public, thereby certifying an ability to at least search for leadership. With each speech act, these certifications mount up, and, with enough of them, it quickly becomes unclear which speech act leads and which only makes pretensions to leadership. The press presumes to help sort out the acts of genuine and feigned leadership, but the press is also caught up in images of rhetoric and war and political power. (ibid., 46)

Why Are Presidents Speaking More Often?

How did this propensity of modern presidents to speak more often but say less come about? According to Carol Gelderman, it was a result of a conscious decision on the part of presidents over time to separate their speechwriters from the policy-making process. Gelderman has written, "From Franklin Delano Roosevelt to Lyndon Baines Johnson, presidents openly used senior aides to help them write speeches. These aides also were actively involved in the policy decisions they helped to communicate" (1997: x).

The speechwriters, furthermore, were "senior aides, who had regular access" to the president (ibid., 74).

Presidents also played an active role in the speechmaking process. As Doris Kearns Goodwin has written,

> Generally, Roosevelt would dictate his thoughts at the end of the day until it was time to go to bed. Then the speechwriters would retire to the large table in the Cabinet Room, where, with scissors and paste, they would begin the task of assembling a coherent speech. The following night, after reading the draft, the president would dictate some more, and then his aides would return to the Cabinet Room to start a second draft. (1994: 238)

The presidents' active role in the speechwriting process, and the active connection between speechwriters and policy making, changed, however, when Richard Nixon assumed the presidency. Gelderman has written,

With Richard Nixon the collaborative process began to break down. For the first time ever, people primarily talented at writing were hired and put on the federal payroll as speechwriters. They needed neither policy expertise nor even knowledge about issues, since they were first and foremost wordsmiths, separated from the president and his policymakers. Divorcing the form of presidential speech (structure and word choice) from its content (policy) has changed the function of the speeches—and to some extent, the very nature of the presidency. (1997: x)

In her important book, *All the Presidents' Words: The Bully Pulpit and the Creation of the Virtual Presidency*, Gelderman has provided numerous examples of how FDR and other modern presidents prior to Richard Nixon integrated speechwriting with policy formulation. The people who wrote the speeches for FDR, Truman, Eisenhower, Kennedy, and Johnson also played an important role in formulating the policies the speeches were about. Furthermore, on more than one occasion, the process of writing the speech had a direct impact on the final policy adopted by a particular administration.

In addition, early in the modern presidency, speeches were more likely to be designed for policy purposes. For example, FDR's "stunning success in mobilizing the nation" prior to U.S. entry into World War II "rested on his notion of the purpose of presidential speechmaking" (ibid., 35). As Samuel Rosenman commented, "More than any other president, perhaps more than any other political figure in history, FDR used the spoken and written word to exercise leadership and carry out policies" (quoted in Gelderman, 35). In other words, speechmaking had a clear purpose: to educate the nation and to lead it in a desired direction.

As Gelderman has noted, "All four presidents" who succeeded Roosevelt "followed in . . . [his] speechwriting footsteps. They adopted his collaborative method by choosing writers from among their top advisers and by recognizing the connection between writing and policymaking." They understood that policy "is made by words . . . and words shape thought" (ibid., 37).

All of this changed, however, with the election of Richard Nixon, who in Chapter 3 we characterized as the first image-is-everything president. "By the time Nixon first ran for president in 1960, fourteen years into 'his political life,' he had developed an unwavering conviction that the perceived image of what a president is and does is far more important than what he actually is or does" (ibid., 76). In an attempt to distance himself from negative images that had evolved during his vice-presidential years and his disastrous run for the governorship of California in 1964, Nixon advertised himself as "the New Nixon" in his 1968 presidential bid. With the help of a slick advertising campaign, Nixon was sold to the American public more like a commodity than a political candidate (see Chapter 4).

Once in the White House, Nixon continued to surround himself with former advertising executives; he was determined to use the same strategy that got him elected to govern the country. He also followed an example begun by his predecessor, Lyndon Johnson, which was to use "specific writers to engender specific images." As the president's "image requirements changed, so did the writers" (Stuckey 1991: 70). For example, for purely political speeches Nixon used William Safire. If, however, he wanted a more combative speech, he relied on Patrick Buchanan. Different speechwriters represented whichever image the president wanted to portray to the public. In short, speechmaking was no longer primarily designed for policy purposes. Nixon now employed it to carefully craft an image of Richard Nixon that could then be sold to the American public. According to one of Nixon's speechwriters, Raymond Price, the Nixon strategy was as follows:

> We have to be very clear on this point: that the response is to the image, not the man, since 99 percent of the voters have no contact with the man. It's not what's there that counts, it's what is projected—and carrying it one step further, it's not what he projects but rather what the voter receives. It's not the man we have to change, but rather the perceived impression. . . . [W]ords are important—but less for what they actually say than for the sense they convey, for the impression they give of the man himself. . . . All this is a roundabout way of getting at the point that we should be concentrating on building a received image of RN [Richard Nixon]. . . . It suggests that we take the time and money to experiment, in a controlled manner, with film and television techniques, with particular emphasis on pinpointing those controlled uses of the television medium that can best convey the image we want to get across. (quoted in Gelderman 1997: 77)

Obviously, a key to the Nixon strategy was the growing importance of television. As radio had provided Franklin Roosevelt with a means of directly communicating with the American public, now television provided a means for presidents to enter the living rooms of average Americans. Unfortunately, as Mary Stuckey has asserted, "As television images dominate, presidential images flatten, become simplified." The reason for this is that television "does not simply mean that presidents talk more. It also means that they talk differently" (1991: 2). Presidents are less likely to speak in a deliberative fashion on television and more likely to emphasize their ceremonial role. In the process, the president becomes "a presenter," and "public argument" is largely supplanted "by public assertion" (ibid., 5). Therefore, as "presidential interpretations have shifted from the long argumentative and premise-laden discourses of earlier years to the visually privileged assertive discourse that characterizes modern televised communication, the American polity is prompted to lose sight of its origins, its philosophical grounding, and its self-understanding" (ibid., 3).

Eisenhower made only limited use of television to govern (for example, taping his press conferences and allowing excerpts to be shown on TV), though he used it widely in his campaigns for the White House. Kennedy became the first true television president. He allowed his press conferences to be broadcast live. In the process, Kennedy came across to the American public as lively, entertaining, knowledgeable, and witty. Never mind that oftentimes there wasn't a great deal of substance to Kennedy's addresses. The point is that on TV Kennedy shone. On the other hand, while the failure of the Johnson administration cannot be tied solely to television, it is clear that TV was not kind to LBJ. His energetic personality, which translated well in one-on-one settings (that is, the famed "Johnson treatment"), did not translate well on television.

Nixon obviously learned a valuable lesson from the Eisenhower, Kennedy, and Johnson presidencies, but he also had much prior experience with television himself. Television saved his political career in 1952. He was Eisenhower's vice-presidential candidate when he was accused of fund-raising improprieties. The story immediately dominated the news, and it appeared that Eisenhower might drop Nixon from the ticket. The Republican National Committee and the Senatorial and Congressional Campaign Committees put up $75,000 to buy one-half hour of television time so that Nixon could personally address the American people (Nixon 1978: 99). In what became known as the "Checkers Speech"—a reference to the Nixon family dog—Nixon defended his ethics in front of a national TV audience. Also watching the speech was Dwight Eisenhower. While Eisenhower initially waffled in response to reporters' questions about Nixon's performance, the public response was overwhelmingly in favor of the young vice-presidential candidate (Nixon 1978: 105–106). And Nixon's political career was thus saved—by the medium of television.

Just eight years later, however, Nixon had a very different experience with television, and learned another important lesson about the medium. In the famous Kennedy-Nixon debates, which Daniel Boorstin (1961) characterized as a pseudo-event, Nixon performed well on substantive debating points. But the audience overwhelmingly favored the young, tanned, good-looking senator from Massachusetts, John F. Kennedy, over the tired, drawn, and five o'clock shadowed face of Richard Nixon. As Nixon later wrote in his memoirs, "Most of the editorial writers based their opinions on substance rather than image, even in the pro-Kennedy *Washington Post*[,] and [the] *St. Louis Post-Dispatch* called the debate a draw, but postdebate polls of the television audience gave the edge to Kennedy" (1978: 219). Nixon continued, "It is a devastating commentary on the nature of television as a political medium that what hurt me the most in the first debate was not the substance of the encounter with Kennedy and me, but the disadvantageous contrast in our physical appearances" (ibid.).

It is not surprising then that as president Nixon placed such an important emphasis on the power of television and image making. Nixon's advisers, Gelderman wrote, "understood better than most in the late 1960s that on television, appearance and manner count for more than substance. Political reality need not correspond to objective reality; a new image was all the reality that counted" (1997: 78).

To define his image, Nixon created a public relations network in the White House. He established the Office of Communications to prepare a "line of the day" that would be provided to the press. In addition, the Office of Public Liaison was established "to feed local, regional, and specialty news organizations outside the Washington press corps" (ibid., 78–79). Nixon also "insisted that his public appearances take place under the most controlled circumstances." The preferred mechanism for this was television. As a result, "[s]peechmaking stood at the apex of his image making; he considered it the most essential duty in his job as chief executive, since it afforded him the opportunity to make his point before the largest number of voters" (ibid., 79–80).

In this process, Nixon compartmentalized policymaking and speechwriting in separate units. No longer would speechwriters be expected to formulate or influence policy. Their job was to promote the president's reputation and image. As a result, a dichotomy developed between substance and image. As Gelderman continued, "Speechmaking like Nixon's, with its public relations emphasis, draws listeners attention away from issues and to the speaker, his ability to speak, and his style of presentation" (1997: 95). As Nixon administration official David Gergen admitted, the president's obsession with his image ultimately resulted in too much distance between his public rhetoric and his deeds (ibid.).

Unfortunately, Nixon's public relations system, once established, became the model for each of his successors. Both Ford and Carter separated their speechwriters from the policy process. While neither president was terribly effective in their use of TV, they did try to take advantage of this medium. It was Ronald Reagan, however, who would make the best use of television. As Gelderman has commented, with "video-age image making, the picture takes precedence over the word" (ibid., 99) and Reagan's advisers were keenly aware of the importance of pictures. Reagan certainly appeared comfortable on television. He was after all both a politician and a former actor, two occupations that when blended together would seem perfect for the media age. As Michael Deaver, Reagan's own "so-called image maker," has written:

> I did not create the label the Great Communicator. I don't know who did. I only know that he ranks with FDR and John Kennedy, in this century as presidents who could deliver a speech with the power to move people. He is, after all, a performer.

The voice is pleasant, the confidence, the timing sharpened by thousands of speeches and scripts. (1987: 76-77)

Reagan's role became that of a "performer," a salesman for his administration's policies; and he was a superb salesman. His administration was equally adept at getting the president's message across. As David Gergen, who served in the Nixon, Reagan, and Clinton administrations, stated, "We wanted to control what people saw, which made daily priorities crystal clear. . . . We would go through the president's schedule day by day and hour by hour and figure out what we wanted the story to be at the end of each day and at the end of each week. And that worked 90% of the time" (quoted in Gelderman 1997: 99). The primary reason for the high success rate was that the Reagan White House gave the television networks what they most wanted: good visual images for their news broadcasts. Ceremonial occasions were best suited for this purpose, since they were less likely to be substantive. In many cases the visual images were all that mattered; not even what the president said mattered. With Reagan the term **photo opportunity** entered the political dictionary. Newscasters soon discovered that so long as the White House controlled the visuals, the White House also controlled the slant of the news. Even if a story was critical of the president, the Reagan White House learned that if the visuals were attractive, the public tended to come away from the story with a positive impression of the president. Image, in its visual context, was now becoming everything. Speechmaking was a mere prop to the visual images. And while substance did not disappear entirely, it was no longer the primary motivation behind presidential speeches or appearances. If a picture could convey a thought, why even worry about the words?

Spin, as in **spin control,** and **sound bite** also entered the political dictionary at this time. When words are important, it is important to make sure that they are coordinated (that is, everyone is saying the same thing). Even before the president gave a particular speech, the administration had written the verdict on the speech for all of its top advisers to present to the media. "The president was brilliant tonight. Relaxed and comfortable. I've never seen him give a speech as good as he did tonight." Such lines were written and memorized long before the speech was actually delivered. Speeches were crafted so that excerpts of 10 seconds or less could be run on the network and local news broadcasts. Catchy phrases for sound bites would be intentionally written into each presidential speech. If the news programs were going to give Reagan 10 seconds or less of air time, his administration wanted to make sure they got the right message—or line—across in that limited time frame. Again, substance was being demoted.

The Reagan White House also became the first to widely use polling and focus groups to evaluate which individual lines would be included or excluded from a particular speech. Reagan's agenda consisted of several clearly articulated, if general, statements about the role of government. For example, he was for smaller government, for getting government off the backs of the people, and for less regulation. He was against abortion and for tax relief. The problem was that while many of these goals were popular in the abstract, they had little public support when, for example, it came to policy specifics, such as cutting individual programs. Consequently, while Reagan's stump speeches were popular, the issues upon which he based his governance often were not. Many people "were put off by Reagan's social agenda, many more by any specific proposals for cuts in the federal budget. And people were particularly afraid of Reagan's designs for Nicaragua" (Mayer and McManus 1988: 203). This led his pollster, Richard Wirthlin, to tell Reagan's speechwriters, "It's the worst issue" (quoted in Mayer and McManus 1988: 203).

Yet these policies "were the core of Reagan's second-term agenda." Still, Wirthlin urged the president's speechwriters to "soft-pedal them and to stress, instead, Reagan's personal promise to cut 'the national budget—not the family budget'" (ibid.). As the speechwriters began to write the president's 1986 State of the Union address, they "were left facing the problem of what else to put into the speech." The answer provided by Michael Deaver, the president's personal image maker, was, "You've got to get something sexy." The speechwriters decided to focus on catastrophic health insurance because Deaver agreed, "Yeah, that's sexy." As one speechwriter later lamented, "It was like sitting around a Madison Avenue advertising agency. It was just nauseating." But when Reagan delivered the speech on February 4, 1986, it was a huge success. Wirthlin noted that the president's poll numbers were better than for any previous State of the Union address. "But the speechwriters, who saw themselves as the keepers of Reagan's ideological flame, were outraged" (ibid., 203–205). Pollsters, not policymakers, had determined the content of the president's speech.

The next year would be no different. Kenneth Khachigian, who had written major speeches for the president before, was put in charge of writing the 1987 State of the Union address. He "quickly discovered that no one could give him any guidance about what the speech should contain" (Mayer and McManus 1988: 371). Later, when a speech was crafted to announce the Strategic Defense Initiative or "Star Wars" antimissile defense system, the speech was "widely tested before focus groups but *not* subjected to policy review" (Gelderman 1997: 102). Consequently, under Reagan, even some of what we have classified here as "major speeches" became nothing more than nonsubstantive exercises in presidential image making. The same was true of some "major speeches" delivered by Bill Clinton. Even substantive speeches often lacked coherence. As Bill Clinton's first labor secretary, Robert Reich, has written, the preparation of the State of the Union address "is like a soccer ball, moving in whichever direction the majority kicks it. If you're not crowded around the ball, kicking like mad, you have no effect on its trajectory" (1997: 70). This method of preparation does not bode well for a coherent expression of a president's political philosophy or for the clear articulation of presidential priorities.

Thus, the following statement by Carol Gelderman on presidential rhetoric is as relevant with regard to "major speeches" as it is to other types of public utterances: "What presidents say is calculated for its effect on their image, an ideal public persona, which is a construct determined by what pollsters say the public admires at any given moment. Presidents' public words no longer aim primarily at reflecting objective reality. Their end is virtual reality—the public presentation of an orchestrated perception" (1997: 115).

Or in Roderick Hart's opinion,

> What used to be a broad, bold line between argument and entertainment, between speech-making and theater, now has no substance at all. Television viewers all too often fail to notice the political fabricating of a presidential speech event or to estimate how hard it was for the president to get the applause he did. Instead, they normally make the simpler discrimination—the president was liked or he was not (1987: 132).

Conclusions

As public speaking has become more important in the modern presidency, "the role of the president in the political system has also changed. The president's function has moved from being one of administration to one of legitimation as the spoken word comes to dominate written text and as electioneering and governing move ever closer together" (Stuckey 1991: 10).

In this chapter we have argued that the propensity toward presidential speech-making has not only increased in recent decades, but that speeches have become less substantive over time. While there are many explanations for this decline in the substance of presidential speeches, the decision to separate speechwriting and policy making clearly has had a major impact. Likewise, television has played an important role. As Bruce Miroff has written, "Television provides the view most amenable to spectacle; by favoring the visual and the dramatic, it promotes stories with simple plot lines over complex analyses of causes and consequences" (1988: 273). Furthermore, a symbiotic relationship has developed between the presidency and television over time. As Theodore Lowi has noted, "what is good for television is the same as what is required for a good plebiscitary presidency," which places the president at the center of the American political system (1985: 114). Unfortunately, the move toward increased speechmaking and increased public appearances has been associated with a concomitant reduction in the actual substance of policy making. Rhetoric is now more often designed to promote a desired presidential image and not to provide leadership for the country.

6

....

Presidential Image and the Media

Despite the president's unprecedented ability to command a media platform, image is a highly volatile quality rapidly undermined by negative coverage.

—Matthew Kerbel, 1995

Bill Clinton (left), Ross Perot (center), and President George Bush share a light moment at the conclusion of the third and final campaign debate, held at Michigan State University. Photo courtesy of Reuters/Mark Cardwell/Archive Photos, reprinted by permission.

··

Who establishes the president's image? From the president's perspective, in a perfect world, presidents and/or their consultants, after conducting various focus groups and surveys, would develop and then sell a desirable image to the public. Such a generic image would undoubtedly include a reputation for toughness (particularly with regard to crime and the international community), fiscal responsibility, decisiveness, political skill, moral integrity, compassion, and so on. Presidents would prefer that the public respond favorably to this image.

Unfortunately for presidents, the process of image creation is much more complicated than this. While presidents and their consultants do indeed try to devise a favorable image for public consumption, rival politicians and other policy makers also try to influence how the public perceives and evaluates the president. Rival politicians have an incentive to portray the president in far less flattering terms than the White House would prefer. For example, Republicans on Capitol Hill have presented a very different image of Bill Clinton than the White House has. While the White House prefers to portray Clinton as decisive and compassionate, congressional Republicans have preferred to describe him as vacillating and shallow. Republicans have characterized Clinton as "Slick Willie" and raised questions about the president's morality (or lack thereof). The White House has, whenever possible, sidestepped issues related to the president's morals and instead focused on the president's deep concern for average Americans.

Such partisan competition is to be expected in a democratic form of government. Even such stellar individuals as George Washington and Dwight Eisenhower had partisan critics who tried to portray them to the public in less than flattering terms. Certainly, Lincoln's political rivals did not describe him as the "Great Emancipator" or as a common man of the people. In the gritty world of Washington politics, there is constant competition over who controls the president's image, just as there is competition over who controls the political agenda. Successful presidents are those able to present the image that they prefer. For example, Ronald Reagan successfully presented an image of toughness, while the Democrats largely failed (at least prior to the Iran-Contra affair) in their attempts to portray the president as a man who was seriously out of touch with the nation's problems. On the other hand, unsuccessful presidents, such as Carter or Bush, have ultimately been defined by their political opposition: Carter as vacillating and ineffective, Bush as out of touch with the needs of ordinary Americans. Somewhere along the way, both men lost control over their own public images.

Presidents and their partisan rivals thus try to define the president's image, but they do not act alone. An important intervening actor is the media—newspapers, magazines, and television. The media do much more than simply report the news. They also interpret it. When they report on news from the White House, or criticisms from Congress or the campaign trail, they also try to tell the American public what the news means. Sometimes they do this intelligently and responsibly, and sometimes not. For our purposes, it is important to note that the media play an integral role in establishing the president's image. In this chapter we will examine how the media interpret and create (or attempt to create) the president's image. We will also examine how the media's role in this process has changed over time. Finally, we will examine how presidents (successful and unsuccessful ones) have attempted to control what the media report.

Part I: The Media Presidency

There was a time when a commander-in-chief was graded on the traditional measures of his relations with Congress, his dealings with foreign leaders, his ability to keep the economy moving and the nation at peace. Now the increasingly opinionated mass media had somehow become the arbiter of political success and the distiller of conventional wisdom. A president's words were endlessly sliced and diced by the self-appointed pundits, his every move filtered through someone else's ideological lens. (Kurtz 1998: xxiv)

In the era of the "constant campaign," controlling the president's or presidential candidate's public image is not only critical to getting elected but also to having the necessary political clout to govern once elected. In this process, presidents must control what the media writes about them. If they do not, they may lose control of their image and the way the public perceives them. This fundamental reality about American politics in the late twentieth century was belatedly learned by President Clinton and his staff. After Clinton was pummeled and bruised during the first half of his first term in office by political controversies generated by the media's coverage of his casual, often impromptu responses to reporters' questions, the White House staff brought in people who understood that none of the president's wide-ranging policy initiatives would succeed unless the White House set the political agenda by seizing the public's attention. They had to manage the news, and to package the presidency in a way that would encourage people to buy the product. To achieve this favorable product packaging, the staff had to engage in a daily struggle with that small coterie of cynical and suspicious journalists, the White House correspondents, who dogged the president's every move and dissected his every utterance. As with Carter, it took only a few days in office for Bill Clinton's media image to change from inspiring leader of a new generation to a politically inept waffler devoid of conviction. His young, amateurish White House staff seemed to be arrogantly ignorant and blissfully disorganized. Throughout the opening weeks of the new administration, normally a honeymoon period for the White House and the media, reporters stressed the president's clumsiness at Washington power politics. From gays in the military to presidential haircuts, Clinton took the media flak and his image suffered. But he seethed in frustration at the media coverage and occasionally vented his anger in well-publicized outbursts at the press.

From the very beginning, then, the normally articulate and charming Bill Clinton developed a sour relationship with the media. It actually began during the 1992 campaign for the Democratic nomination. The press's focus on charges of the candidate's marital infidelity, draft evasion, and marijuana smoking was deeply resented by Clinton and his wife. Throughout the 1992 campaign, Clinton had considerable success circumventing the mainstream press and going directly to the voters with cable TV interviews and electronic town hall meetings. Upon entering the presidency, Clinton thought he could continue this evasive approach. The White House closed staff offices to reporters, made it known that press conferences would be infrequent, and limited interviews with top administration officials. These efforts to control the message and manage the news were perceived by the media as clumsy at best. But Clinton underestimated the power of the press. As Kurtz recounts, the White House reporters who were feeling bypassed and manipulated struck back.

> The small group of journalists who shouted questions each day in the White House Briefing Room had a very different agenda. They were focused, almost fixated, on scandal, on the malfeasance and misfeasance and plain old embarrassments that had seemed to envelop this administration from the very start. They were interested in conflict, in drama, in behind-the-scenes maneuvering, in pulling back the curtain and exposing Oz-like manipulations of the Clinton crowd. It was their job to report what the President said, but increasingly they saw it as their mission to explain why he said it and what seedy political purpose he was trying to accomplish along the way. (Kurtz 1998, xix)

Thus, a daily struggle developed between the White House staff, who sought to package the presidency in a way that people would buy the product, and the reporters, bent on churning out scandalous news. Sensing a failed presidency, Clinton reorganized his staff midway through his first term and then again at the beginning of the second term, adding ever more seasoned political and press operatives to his inner circle. It was a staff that became increasingly adept at spin control as it gained experience by dealing with a seemingly endless series of crises and scandals. There were the foreign policy quagmires of Somalia, Bosnia, and Haiti; the Justice Department and special prosecutor investigating the Whitewater real estate development scheme; "travel-gate"; misuse of confidential FBI files; campaign fund-raising excesses; and the alleged improprieties of several Cabinet officers. But the "spinmeisters," whose carefully honed media strategy worked successfully to deflect damaging news and to create a favorable image of the president, faced their ultimate challenge in the revelations of Clinton's sexual peccadilloes that emerged from the Paula Jones sexual harassment civil suit. Jones' lawyers produced depositions from a string of women reporting sexual involvements that ranged from consensual affairs to uninvited and offensive advances. The revelation that sparked a media firestorm, though, involved a former White House intern named Monica Lewinsky.

On January 7, 1998, after having been subpoenaed in the Paula Jones case, Monica Lewinsky gave a deposition in which she denied having any sexual relationship with President Clinton. For months before the deposition, she had been regaling her friend and confidant, Linda Tripp, with tales of a romantic relationship with Bill Clinton that began during her White House internship and involved telephone calls, exchanges of gifts, and oral sex. Ms. Tripp reported the conversations with Lewinsky to the Independent Counsel, Kenneth Starr, when she learned that Lewinsky intended to lie about her relationship with the president. Tripp described phone conversations that she had taped in which Lewinsky implied that she had engaged in sex with President Clinton and had received numerous phone calls from him. After agreeing to cooperate with the Independent Counsel, Ms. Tripp was supplied with an audio recording device by the FBI; she then met with Ms. Lewinsky for four hours, during which time Ms. Lewinsky repeated many of her earlier revelations. The Independent Counsel negotiated with Ms. Lewinsky, seeking her testimony regarding her relationship with the president and any counsel he gave her. By mid-January a special federal court, acting on the recommendation of Attorney General Janet Reno, broadened the Independent Counsel's investigative authority to include accusations that Clinton and presidential friend Vernon Jordan may have encouraged Ms. Lewinsky to lie. On January 17, 1998, President Clinton was questioned for six hours by lawyers for Paula Jones. It was subsequently revealed that he had admitted having an affair with Gennifer Flowers but denied all other accusations of sexual advances or involvement, including those with Monica Lewinsky. Finally, *Newsweek* broke the Lewinsky story in the February 2, 1998 issue, which was released in late January. In it a total of ten articles, covering 34 pages, detailed the stories and rumors of sex, lies, the president, Monica Lewinsky, Linda Tripp, and Kathleen Willey (a sometime White House volunteer who reported being fondled by President Clinton while they were in his private study off the Oval Office). Media reaction was immediate: the Lewinsky story dominated all news coverage in the print and broadcast media and on the Internet. The pope's historic visit to Cuba, once described by Dan Rather of *CBS News* as the most important story of the year, was relegated to the back pages and was largely ignored by television. In fact, the evening news network anchors who were in Cuba to report on the papal visit all rushed back to the U.S. to report on the unfolding sex scandal. Rumor and erroneous information from frequently unnamed sources were reported as facts as journalists rushed to publicize the latest salacious details. The traditional "two sources" rule was abandoned, and the stories became richly embellished with each retelling as reporters sought to maximize the prurient appeal or to imply that there was official intrigue designed to cover up criminal misbehavior. *Newsweek*'s February 9 issue devoted 12 articles and 32 pages to the alleged scandal and admitted that "this is a controversy built for the age of O.J. [Simpson], in which law, politics and entertainment merge into one cable-ready obsession" (p. 25). Emblematic of the media frenzy was *Time*'s special report in its February 16, 1998, issue entitled "The Press and the Dress: the anatomy of a salacious leak, and how it ricocheted around the walls of the media echo chamber." In the article Adam Cohen wrote:

> In a story with no shortage of lurid details, news that Monica Lewinsky may have kept a dress stained from sex with President Clinton was in a class by itself. For fans of the prurient, it offered the tale of a woman so smitten by a sexual encounter that she vowed to keep the most unseemly of souvenirs. For the prosecution-minded, it promised hard DNA evidence. And for those hoping to see the powerful humbled, it introduced a pulse-racing new phrase: Presidential semen. (p. 52)

Cohen relates that the story of the "sex dress" originated in cyberspace. On January 21, Matt Drudge reported on his Internet *Drudge Report* that Linda Tripp had told investigators Lewinsky had confided that she "kept a garment with Clinton's dried semen on it—a garment she allegedly said she would never wash." Drudge did not identify his sources but said, "I know it to be a black cocktail dress." NBC gave Drudge credibility by letting him tell his story on the *Today* show. Then ABC's Jackie Judd quoted on *World News Tonight* "an unnamed source saying Monica Lewinsky saved a navy blue dress stained with President Clinton's semen." Cohen went on for three pages describing the various media reports that characterized the "sex dress" as a black cocktail dress or a navy blue dress or a stained undergarment. Yet the FBI found no evidence of a semen-stained garment among

Lewinsky's clothes and William Ginsburg, Lewinsky's attorney, flatly denied the existence of the "sex dress." The dress, however, was later produced by Ms. Lewinsky, who had given it to her mother for safekeeping. While the dress did indeed exist, the reports of its existence in February 1998 were based on the most tenuous of evidence. Nonetheless, even the most reputable print and broadcast media continued for a week to carry what was then an unsubstantiated story. Cohen defends the media in writing: "The truth does not always emerge immediately or neatly in a story this difficult and fast-paced. It will take still more time before the remaining wrinkles in the story of the dress get ironed out. If it ever happens at all" (*Time*, p. 54).

The press also reported unsubstantiated allegations that President Clinton and Vernon Jordan had coached Monica Lewinsky on lying, thus engaging in suborning perjury and obstruction of justice. Many writers mused that these are impeachable offenses and speculated about the end of the Clinton presidency. But the public did not share the media's moral outrage, demonstrating that they were willing to wait for the facts to develop. Indeed, in the midst of the Lewinsky furor, Clinton's approval rating soared to 70 percent, the highest rating of his presidency. (*Wall Street Journal*, February 6, 1998: A24) Further, the public was turned off by a media coverage of the alleged affair that seemed preoccupied with prurient detail. Geneva Overholser, the *Washington Post*'s ombudsman, wrote an op-ed piece that appeared on January 30, 1998, reporting the reactions of readers to the *Post*'s coverage.

> We don't care about President Clinton's sex life, said the callers. We knew he
> played around. Presidents often have had unsavory private lives. We care that
> the nation is in good shape. We're tired of these constant investigations,
> these constant attempts to bring him down.

Syndicated columnist David Broder took his fellow journalists to task over their excessive concern with the sexual behavior of prominent politicians. Broder wrote, "Perhaps a cadre of candidates of impeccable morals awaits. Until then, the press ought to exercise some restraint and try harder to put these matters in perspective. The public is choking on a surfeit of smut" (*Albuquerque Journal*, January 27, 1998: A12).

Meanwhile, at the White House, the spinmeisters, led by the First Lady, Hillary Rodham Clinton, developed a media strategy based on the premise that the best defense is a good offense. The president forcefully denied the allegations of an involvement with Lewinsky: "I did not have sexual relations with that woman" (Press conference on January 26, 1998). Mrs. Clinton said on national television that she believed her husband, and that the story was part of an orchestrated effort by right-wing conservatives to discredit Bill Clinton and his presidency. The White House staff reiterated all the denials, stonewalled all requests for additional information, stressed the remarkable performance of the economy and lauded the president's State of the Union address. The president kept to his work and travel schedule and seemingly ignored the threatening scandal. The strategy worked. The public excused the president and criticized the media for irresponsible reporting. The reaction of the media, especially the television news pundits, was to engage in self-criticism about the excessive reporting of prurient detail and the failure to substantiate the "facts" of their stories. Yet, the White House press corps was stunned by the public's willingness to overlook President Clinton's morally lax, if not patently offensive, behavior as revealed in the testimony given during the Paula Jones civil suit, and its readiness to criticize the press for reporting the sexual encounters. The favorable image of the president as a competent policy maker in managing the economy, caring for the disadvantaged, and maintaining international peace outweighed the image of Bill Clinton as a man of seriously flawed character. The White House beat the press in this early round of the "image game," at the same time proving that the president's public image is not created solely by the media.

Part II: Evolution of the Press

While recent presidents have had a more confrontational relationship with the media, all presidents have sought a favorable public image, not only to get elected or reelected but to enhance their ability to govern. Until well into the twentieth century the president's image was most heavily influenced by newspapers. For most of the Republic's first century, newspapers were intensely partisan, and their publishers and editors had few qualms about sacrificing objectivity or truth in support of their party's candidates or office-holders. The newspapers were either owned outright by political parties or were supported by their patronage. Government printing contracts went to the newspapers that supported the president.

As Matthew Kerbel notes in his 1995 book *Remote and Controlled: Media Politics in a Cynical Age*, "The present tendency to rake political figures over the coals has deep roots in American history"(29). George Washington was the first target of newspaper abuse and ridicule. It began during the Revolutionary War when the Tory opposition tried to subvert the American war effort. Despite his popularity as a war leader and the unanimity of his election as president of the United States, Washington was the recipient of both extravagant praise and virulent criticism from the most partisan press any president has ever faced. This circumstance is vividly described by Tebbel and Watts in their book *The Press and the Presidency.*

> Ironically Washington, the idol of the nation, and Jefferson, the prime architect and unyielding upholder of press freedom, suffered most from a press that was now free to publish anything short of libel (a law not often invoked by politicians in those days). They were fated to rehearse nearly all the problems that were to plague the relationship between press and president from that time onward to our own. For Washington, it was particularly difficult to be so enmeshed because it had been his policy from the beginning to hold aloof from direct contact with the press as much as possible. But the press would have none of it. There has never been a time in journalistic history when newspapers were so noisily partisan, so utterly unrestrained in their language. There was not even the pretense of objectivity; newspapers were either under the direct control of party politicians or were totally committed to one side of the argument. (1985: 9–10)

In correspondence to friends, Washington expressed his view that the press was disturbing "the peace of the community." Whether newspapers attacked him or defended him, the result was a further polarization of the nation that he had hoped to unite. But Washington was a believer in "managed news," and he did use the press to his own political advantage whenever possible (ibid., 10).

The virulent personal attacks and blatant partisanship appealed to the lowest common denominator among newspaper readers and sold newspapers. As technology changed, lowering the costs of mass printing and distribution, circulation became ever larger in the nineteenth century, and partisan attacks were gradually replaced by sex and scandal—sensational stories—as a means of selling papers. As Richard Davis has observed, "The partisan press, at its peak during the Jacksonian era, gradually would be replaced by a press governed by journalistic and economic, rather than political, considerations and engaged in a more egalitarian relationship with politicians and a more autonomous role within the political system" (1996: 31).

A turning point in American journalism was the introduction of the *New York Sun* into the newspaper industry in 1833. The *Sun* sold for one penny and relied on street sales, while its competitors relied on annual subscriptions that cost about six cents a copy. The *Sun* appealed to a mass readership not only because it was affordable but also because of its content. Since the Revolutionary period, American newspapers had been written to provide political and business information to the political and commercial elite, not to interest the average citizen.

> Although politics remained a major component, the new newspapers featured other topics in news and opinion as well, in accordance with heightened public interest. Nonpolitical stories featured human interest, crime, sex scandals, sports, social events, and other items. News in the penny papers was culled from the police blotter,

public trials, events in the street, and any other activities which might conceivably be of interest. Stories were written as much to entertain as to inform; they rarely focused on weighty issues. (ibid., 36)

The *Sun* was a financial success due principally to its large readership, which attracted lucrative advertising from the manufacturers of the newly available mass-produced consumer goods. The newspapers that adopted the *Sun*'s format and marketing strategy also prospered. The penny press was freed from dependence on political parties and government contracts. As the number of daily newspapers in the United States mushroomed, from less than 400 in 1853 to 2,400 in 1903, the dailies became reliant on circulation and advertising, not government patronage (ibid., 42). To broaden circulation the newspapers not only increased the nonpolitical editorial content but began to downplay partisan bias; they sought to appeal to readers beyond just one set of partisan identifiers. Further, the professionalization of journalism that accompanied larger news-gathering staffs and the nationalization of news coverage made possible by the invention of the telegraph produced an advocacy for "independent journalism." It became clear that nonpartisan, objective reporting sold more news stories for the wire services and more copies for the newspapers. By the end of the nineteenth century, the press was driven by commercial concerns rather than narrow partisan political concerns. This would prove useful to a president like Theodore Roosevelt, who was interested in advancing a new action-oriented image of the presidency (see Chapter 2).

The competition for ever greater circulation led to changes in the nature of news reporting, types of feature articles, and the newspaper format. News content and presentation were changed to emphasize sensationalism and entertainment rather than information. William Randolph Hearst, the publisher of the *New York Journal*, is quoted as admitting "It is the *Journal*'s policy to engage brains as well as to get the news, for the public is even more fond of entertainment than it is of information" (ibid., 46). The commercial competition ushered in an era in journalistic history that saw what is called "yellow journalism." The human interest story was still the staple of news content, as it had been since the advent of the penny press. The worst of yellow journalism, however, was characterized by excessiveness—"scare headlines in bold black type, full-page line drawings and illustrations, heavy black or red borders, and highly dramatized text. Shocking headlines were designed to grab reader attention" (ibid., 45).

These excesses were criticized sharply by civic groups, religious leaders, and editors of non-yellow newspapers, yet some yellow press innovations have survived to this day—full-color Sunday supplements, lengthy feature articles, popular comic sections, use of pictures, and occasional banner headlines. Following the age of yellow journalism, political news had to be packaged in new formats in order to be compatible with the rest of the newspaper content and to be palatable to the new readers. Politicians could no longer depend on the favorable reporting of their speeches and actions by captive newspapers. The large elite dailies needed "a steady generation of news with color and drama, predictable sources of news, and ready access to those available sources" (ibid., 52). Thus, in order to manipulate the press into portraying them favorably, presidents had to now develop what we presently call "media strategies."

Although magazines and journals devoted to reporting and commenting on politics and government have existed since the early days of the Republic, their readership has been restricted and segmented. These publications have usually targeted the political and economic elite, not the mass public.

Newspapers were the dominant media of political communication until the invention of the radio. Technological developments made widespread commercial radio broadcasting possible by the late 1920s, and once again the relationship between the news media and politicians was altered. It was now possible for the president to speak directly to a nationwide audience and bypass the intervening communication screen of reporters and editors. Yet, to be effective at using the radio for political communication, presidents had to change their speaking form from lengthy addresses delivered with oratorical flourish to relatively short, direct messages delivered in a pleasing, well-modulated voice. As we noted in Chapter 5, Franklin Roosevelt was the first president to master the new medium.

Radio broadcasting began as a private enterprise, and Congress decided early on that it should remain largely a privately owned industry. In most other countries, radio broadcasting was state-owned or state-controlled. Yet, even in the United States it quickly became clear that government must play a regulatory role to avoid frequency interference and other technical difficulties. Advocates of regulation argued that the airwaves belonged to the public and that broadcasting should be regulated like a utility—in the public's interest. The regulation of broadcasting content, however, could amount to censorship, which would be in violation of the constitutional guarantees of free speech and a free press, and such regulation, therefore, has been the subject of intense policy debate. The result has been that government intervention in programming has been rare, and when it has occurred it has involved issues of obscenity, not politics. Government regulation has not impinged on the autonomy of the press. Private ownership of the broadcast media has meant that commercial concerns dominate programming and news coverage. Radio broadcasters have been as intent on entertaining their listeners as the popular press journalists have been in entertaining their readers.

Providing political information has been of secondary importance for both media in the modern era. Thus, the radio did not displace newspapers but rather became a supplemental information source. Consequently, radio in both electoral politics and governance has played the role of an additional and/or alternative vehicle for political communication.

Adding pictures to the sound transmissions has had a major impact on news coverage and once again altered the nature of the interaction between reporters and politicians. Television puts a premium on the *visual* depiction of people and events. Pictures dominate the communication. The dramatic potential of moving images and live coverage means that sensational and emotional news coverage has far exceeded the most ardent efforts (and aspirations) of the penny press journalists. Despite the potential for the medium to offend its audience, government regulation of television has not been significantly more intrusive than it has been for radio. In fact, the regulations and rules governing television have been largely extensions of those promulgated for radio. Public ownership or subsidy of radio and television stations did not become meaningful until the establishment of the Corporation for Public Broadcasting in 1967. Public broadcasting programming appears to appeal to only a small elite audience. It is the privately owned television stations that dominate broadcasting. Private ownership for commercial purposes means that the objective of all management decisions is to make a profit—and television is a lucrative business. It is the public's near universal access to television that makes the broadcasting industry work. Nearly 99 percent of American households have at least one television set. The marketing potential of such a vast audience is stupendous, as Stephen Ansolabehere and his colleagues have noted in their book *The Media Game*.

> Television's enormous viewership represents millions of consumers who can be wooed through advertising. The broadcasters—the local stations, networks, and cable companies—are in a sense intermediaries. They develop, distribute, and broadcast programming designed to attract as large an audience as possible, and then sell access to that audience to advertisers. (1993: 12)

Americans watch television an average of four hours per day (Ansolabehere et al., 1993: 13) and receive most of their information about public affairs from television news coverage. Studies have shown that fully 50 million people watch one of the three traditional network news shows daily, and 80 percent of the adult population reports that television news is their primary source of political information (Alger 1996: 69). No daily newspaper has a circulation greater than 2 million, although 100 million people claim to read some newspaper every day (Ansolabehere 1993: 41). Getting political information from newspapers requires the ability to read; no such skill is required to watch television. Consequently, those citizens with less education are most likely to learn what they know about public affairs from television. On the other hand, the consumers of information from multimedia sources (newspapers, magazines, radio, conversation with friends and associates) are most likely to be in the upper economic and social classes. Increasingly, however, television is the news source of choice for most Americans. It has become an all-important and influential intermediary between the individual and society and between citizens and politicians; consequently, "making the news" in a favorable light is critical for both office-seekers and officeholders. Those who shape the content of television news (such as a successful president) also influence how Americans think about politics. Managing the news and controlling their public image is even more important for politicians today than it was in the past, but their strategy and tactics must be compatible with the commercial objectives of the modern media.

Part III: Controlling the Media—The Early Presidents

How then do successful presidents control the media? Since its creation, presidents have kept a watchful eye on the media and what it reports. George Washington initially subscribed to five newspapers and three magazines as a means of gauging public opinion. As his presidency continued, the number of periodicals he read on a regular basis increased to about thirty. Washington read so many periodicals because he was deeply concerned about the public's impressions and expectations of him. In a letter to Edward Rutledge, Washington wrote, "I fear, if the issue of public measures should not correspond with their sanguine expectations, they will turn the extravagant (and I may say undue) praises which they are heaping upon me at this moment, into equally extravagant (that I will fondly hope unmerited) censures" (quoted in Tebbel and Watts 1985: 9). Washington's correspondence with Rutledge may in fact show the first expression of what presidential scholars have subsequently called the "expectations gap."

Washington's immediate successor, John Adams, was also the victim of attacks from the opposition press. By the time of Adams' presidency, the Federalist Party had come to believe "that the opposition press represented a seditious threat to their continuance in power, and, therefore, to the stability of the government and the Constitution." As a result, a Sedition Law was enacted that "made it a crime to print material critical of government leaders." The editors of several opposition-party-run newspapers (the Republican Party being the opposition) were subsequently prosecuted under the new law's terms (Sharp 1993: 218).

The Sedition Law threatened the basic tenets of free speech, as well as the idea of a free press. It is therefore fortunate that the law was repealed following the election of Thomas Jefferson in 1800. This election ushered in a period of greater toleration for opposition newspapers, one which Jefferson would, at times, have reason to regret. It was the Federalist press that first widely disseminated the story (or news, depending on one's perspective) that Jefferson had an affair with one of his slaves (Sally Hemmings) and, as a result, had fathered an illegitimate child. In fact, as Tebbel and Watts noted, "There were times . . . when" Jefferson "appeared to speak against the press, and against his principle" of a free press, "but those words rose out of the disappointment, anger, and frustration he felt when the newspapers of his time failed so abysmally to match his ideals" (1985: 29–30).

Jefferson had his own method of controlling the media. He did it not by enacting restrictive legislation, but by filing libel actions "in states where they were most likely to succeed.*" In so doing, Jefferson hoped to "put the fear of the law into the other papers so that they would restrain themselves." He preferred this selective process instead of a general prosecution so that he would "leave his public image unblemished—an early triumph of public relations" (ibid., 33). In fact, Jefferson, and his successor, James Madison, viewed the manipulation of the press "as a primary means for reaching the public, and, in a manner of all presidents, they did not hesitate to manipulate it in whatever way they could. It was the bare beginning of what has become an art in our time, as government has become ever more powerful" (ibid., 44).

Of our early presidents, the first real master of press manipulation was undoubtedly Andrew Jackson. Jackson was the first president to have, essentially, his own personal presidential newspaper. This allowed him to get his ideas across to the American public in an unfettered form. Jackson's close personal friend, Amos Kendall (editor of *The Argus of the Western World*), wrote down the president's thoughts, "often as the president lay back on a couch and smoked his pipe." Later, Kendall and Francis Blair (the editor of the *Globe*) "would write, or rewrite, what the president had said into stories for the Globe." This proved to be a "highly profitable partnership for everyone concerned, through both the Jackson administrations and Martin Van Buren's, as well." In this manner, Jackson "emerged as the first presidential manipulator of the press, in a practical, systematic way that far surpassed any earlier attempts" (ibid., 81).

Despite all of these early attempts to control the media, however, presidents had only limited success. Part of the problem was that the newspapers of this time, as we have noted, were hardly interested in the art of objective reporting. Newspapers were often created specifically for the purpose of representing the views of a particular political party. Papers loyal to the president promoted the president's party and its stand on the issues, berated the opposition party, and promoted the president's image and reputation. Meanwhile, the opposition party newspapers attacked the president, his policies, and his followers. Often, the level of reporting was nothing shy of scurrilous.

Perhaps no president in the history of the United States had less success in controlling what the media reported about him than did Abraham Lincoln, who, ironically, is generally regarded as our nation's greatest president. Lincoln temporarily shut down several newspapers during the early months of the Civil War (Mitgang 1989: xi), an act he no doubt believed was necessary in order to advance his larger goal: to save the Union. It is unclear if this act had any effect on subsequent press coverage of our sixteenth president, but the press portrayed Lincoln as a bumbling oaf. It regularly accused him of being a dictator and criticized his actions as commander-in-chief. Some thought he was not doing enough to advance the Union cause, while others criticized him for unduly expanding presidential power. His views on race and slavery also were examined in critical detail. Even actions that today are heralded were subject to intense press criticism. For example, when Lincoln announced the Emancipation Proclamation, the highly partisan *Chicago Tribune* responded on September 24, 1862:

Two days ago the President was wonderfully strong in the confidence of the country, not because of his military conduct of the war, for, in the opinion of all men, that had been disastrous, but because he had steadily manifested an apparently inflexible determination to adhere faithfully to the constitution in the political management of the war and in the general administration of the government. It was the merit of this adherence that, in the minds of all good and right-thinking men, covered his multitude of sins in the military conduct of the war. So long as he seemed to be fast-anchored to the constitution, good and right thinking men never ceased to hope and believe that experience would teach him to correct and overcome his military mistakes, and that finally the government of the constitution would prevail over rebellion, and that the Union would be established.

Now that he has cut loose from the constitution—now that he has resorted to the same higher law than the constitution for the professed purpose of suppressing the rebellion by which the rebellion justifies itself—good and right thinking men know not what to think or believe, or whither to turn for anchorage. They are smitten with a sense of alarm and dismay. They feel that the foundations of the government are unsettled, if not broken up—that the ship is adrift without master, compass or rudder, and that the chances of wreck are vastly greater than of safety.

If the policy of the proclamation were any more defensible than the President's constitutional power to issue it, the shadows which it has cast over the land would not be so impenetrable. It is an act of as bad faith to every conservative man in the North as it is a terrible blow to the Union men of the border slave States. . . .

We protest against the proclamation, in the name of the constitution, in behalf of good faith to the conservative millions of the northern and border States, and for the sake of the only means by which it has at any time been possible to restore the Union. We protest against it as a monstrous usurpation, a criminal wrong, and an act of national suicide. (quoted in Mitgang 1989: 303–304)

Lincoln's greatest moment as president was thus dismissed by a northern newspaper (though one that had never been a supporter of Lincoln or his policies) from his own home state. While Lincoln ultimately prevailed over such vicious media attacks in the eyes of history, it would not be until the twentieth century that presidents would develop sophisticated techniques for controlling the media.

Part IV: Controlling the Media During the Early Twentieth Century

As we have noted, by the dawn of the twentieth century, the nature of the newspaper business was beginning to change. In the mid-1800s national news services such as the Associated Press (AP) had begun to emerge. The AP and other news services (for example, United Press International [UPI]) would fundamentally change the way news was reported. Prior to their existence, news reporting was largely a parochial affair. Newspapers were tailored for a particular local audience. A politician could express one opinion to a newspaper in one part of a state, and another, contrary opinion to a newspaper in another part of the same state, with minimal fear that he would be held accountable for these divergent statements. Presidents thus had an incentive to speak to local audiences rather than to the nation as a whole. With the emergence of the AP, however, reporting moved to the national level. Presidents found that their ability to send mixed messages to the electorate had been compromised.

The first president to understand the changing media dynamics was Theodore Roosevelt, who assumed the presidency in 1901 upon the assassination of William McKinley. As we noted in Chapter 2, Teddy Roosevelt skillfully used the media to promote a favorable image of himself to the American people. When he assumed the presidency, Roosevelt already had a rudimentary model for his media relations. During McKinley's presidency, Dan Lamont, the administration's White House Secretary, had "realized that to reach the public on behalf of the President he had to find ways to provide the press with a continuous flow of news. He needed to supply reporters with appropriate information in time for them to meet their deadlines, and to do so in a way that also would help the President" (Grossman and Kumar 1981: 21).

Lamont's efforts were hampered by the fact that McKinley was a rather color-less individual; it was difficult to evoke much public interest in him. On the other hand, Teddy Roosevelt was a reporter's dream come true. Young, flamboyant, dashing, colorful: these are but a few of the adjectives that described the new pres-ident. In other words, Teddy Roosevelt was definitely newsworthy. A still small but growing Washington press corps was hungry for news about the president, and Teddy Roosevelt was smart enough to realize that he could use this favorable press coverage to advance his political aspirations. His secretary, William Loeb, Jr., "continued the practice of providing 'guidance' for reporters by issuing state-ments and press releases, answering questions at regular but informal meetings, and providing reporters with stories when their deadlines required that they have something" (Grossman and Kumar 1981: 22).

Roosevelt also personally invited reporters into the inner White House sanctu-ary for personal interviews, often off the record. During these encounters Teddy Roosevelt expressed whatever opinions were on his mind, often in colorful terms that translated into exceedingly good print. Thankful for their insider's view of the presidency, reporters responded with generally favorable coverage of the new president. Through this synergistic process, Roosevelt was able to largely control what the media reported about him, while newspapers benefited by their soaring subscription rates.

Teddy Roosevelt's innovative technique, however, was largely dependent on a sympathetic and small coterie of reporters. Within just a few decades of Teddy Roosevelt's presidency, however, the nature of the Washington press corps had changed dramatically. It grew both larger and more skeptical of presidential pro-nouncements. While Teddy Roosevelt's successors continued to use a White House secretary as a liaison with the press, Herbert Hoover was the first to limit his assistant's (George Akerson) duties to "making appointments and maintain-ing press relations." Still, as Richard Stout of the *Christian Science Monitor* later commented, "Akerson and [his successor Theodore] Joslin were not spokesmen for the President but merely giving you information about the activities of the President" (Grossman and Kumar 1981: 22).

It was Franklin Delano Roosevelt (FDR) who reinvented press relations. His secretary, Stephen Early, "quickly made it apparent that he was going to do more than inform reporters about the activities of the President." As Richard Stout commented, "The whole administration was a public relations effort, and Early was right in the middle of it" (Grossman and Kumar 1981: 23). As Grossman and Kumar noted, "In the Roosevelt administration, when the skills of the President as communicator became more critical to his success, a press secretary emerged who played an important role as his public relations manager" (ibid.). While FDR did not always have warm relations with the press (see Best 1993), his media innovations did serve as a model for future presidents.

By the time FDR was elected to the presidency, another revolutionary addition to the media had already appeared: broadcast radio. Although politicians before Roosevelt had tended to speak on the radio as if they were addressing a large convention hall, Franklin Roosevelt instinctively knew that he was really speaking to Americans who were sitting in their homes. Roosevelt took advantage of the intimacy of radio to speak directly to each individual American. No longer did a president have to worry about how a speech would be interpreted by the press. Now the people could hear the speech, and the president, for themselves. They could hear the confidence in his voice, the subtle inflections that are easily lost when the word is reduced to print.

FDR had access to this powerful new technology, but he used it sparingly. He realized that if he were to go on the air too often, the public would grow tired of his addresses. He therefore limited the number of "Fireside Chats" to approximately two per year. These speeches thus became events that were sure to be listened to by a wide audience. Radio also allowed Roosevelt to go over the heads of the press and other Washington insiders, to address the public directly and uncensored. Roosevelt's successors quickly learned the power of radio and, later, television. Unfortunately, as presidents speak more and more (see Chapter 5), they apparently have forgotten Roosevelt's more important lesson: If one speaks too often, one will wear out one's welcome with the American people.

Part V: Press Relations in the Image-Is-Everything Era

Franklin Roosevelt's successors continued to seek innovative ways to control the media. Dwight Eisenhower was the first president to use TV commercials in a political campaign. He also was the first president to tape his press conferences, although only excerpts were then provided to the television networks. Eisenhower hired actor Robert Montgomery to give him lessons on public speaking. He named James Hagerty as his Press Secretary, thus further elevating and clarifying that post (Raichur and Waterman 1993: 4).

As we noted in Chapter 5, John Kennedy became the first true TV president. He was the first to televise his press conferences live. This proved to be the perfect forum for his wit and verbal acuity. And Kennedy not only sounded good on television, he also looked good. From Franklin Roosevelt's time onward, it became necessary for presidents to be good public speakers and to have a clear message. From Kennedy's presidency onward, the public came to expect presidents to look and sound good on TV. The problem with this expectation is that not all presidents are good public speakers and many do not look comfortable on television. Thomas Jefferson was a shy man who had an occasional stutter. Abraham Lincoln, though he was known as a great orator, apparently had a high-pitched voice and was hardly telegenic in appearance. Probably neither man would have looked or sounded good on television, which raises an important point: As the nature of the media has changed over time, public expectations have changed as well. Today, we expect our presidents to be able to communicate effectively with us. Sadly, deliberation and intelligence, once highly regarded qualities, are not rewarded as much as a steady voice or a comforting appearance. Television has had much to do with this transition in public expectations.

Grossman and Kumar have written, "The most conspicuous changes in the relationship between the White House and news organizations since the 1950s can be traced to the growing perception by White House officials that television is the most important medium for the President to dominate" (1981: 28). In fact, Grossman and Kumar noted that during the Carter administration, most White House staffers seemed to gear their activities exclusively toward television, as if it was the only media outlet. Because presidents have geared their activities toward television, recent presidents, especially the more successful ones, have paid considerable attention to how they look on television. Controlling the media in the television age has thus become one of controlling physical appearance, as well as controlling the message.

As we noted in the last chapter, lacking Kennedy's good looks, charm, presence, and his sense of humor, Lyndon Johnson and Richard Nixon had to find other methods of controlling the media. Johnson was not successful. As Grossman and Kumar (1981: 45) wrote, "During the 1960s television became the battleground in what the public perceived as a war between the presidency and the media. It was television news that carried the message to the American people that Lyndon Johnson's efforts in Vietnam were not going well." Following Johnson, Nixon was determined to do a better job of controlling the media. It is too easy to remember only Watergate and thus forget that for a substantial period of time, Nixon succeeded in that endeavor.

The basic form of Nixon's method has been used by all subsequent successful presidents. Nixon established a sophisticated public relations operation in the White House. The line between policy and pseudo-events often became blurred. The public relations opportunities of such major policy events as détente with the Soviet Union and the opening to China became as important as the policy initiatives themselves. The president's trips to the Soviet Union and China were orchestrated to provide good visuals for the television networks, and thus for the viewing public at home. Nixon didn't simply meet with the Chinese leadership, he visited the Great Wall of China. The idea was to present the president in highly telegenic settings that made him look presidential. These televised events did much to bolster Nixon's stature as a great statesman and to convince the American public that he was worthy of reelection.

Nixon also used television effectively to speak to the nation. While his speaking style was stilted, his approval ratings increased substantially following his major address to the nation on Vietnam, popularly known as his "Silent Majority" speech. Had not Watergate intervened, Nixon's use of the media might be perceived in much more positive terms today, even given the negative press he received during the Vietnam War. Ironically, Nixon's obsessive suspicion (even hatred) of the press contributed to his ultimate downfall. Nixon was particularly suspicious of what he called the "Eastern Establishment press," which consisted of such papers as the *Washington Post*, the *New York Times*, and even the *St. Louis Post Dispatch* (Kutler 1997: 163). When the *Washington Post* in 1972 ran stories about the emerging Watergate affair, Nixon told an aide, John Ehrlichman, "There ain't going to be no forgetting, and there'll be Goddamn little forgiving, except they're going to know (unintelligible). They're off the guest list, they don't come to the Christmas party." Nixon then discussed using the Federal Communications Commission to go after TV licenses held by the *Post* (Kutler 1997: 174–75). It is these excesses we remember today, that and the spectacle of a disgraced president resigning from office. But prior to his self-destruction, Nixon provided a valuable lesson to future politicians of both parties on how to control what the media reports. He institutionalized media relations in the White House and made public relations an integral component of the president's policy-making apparatus.

Both Gerald Ford and Jimmy Carter failed in their attempts to use television to their advantage. But Ronald Reagan came to the White House with the perfect training for a politician in the television age. He had been an actor as well as a successful state governor. He knew from training and experience the importance of the camera. Reagan also appointed a number of former Nixon aides to the White House. They had learned the techniques of presidential salesmanship and control of the media during Nixon's presidency. Under Reagan, they developed these techniques into a veritable art form. As Nixon was photographed on the Great Wall of China, Reagan was photographed, for example, at the Statue of Liberty, overlooking Normandy beach, at the Demilitarized Zone (the DMZ) in Korea, and in other such settings. The press was now allowed to photograph the president, but not to ask him any questions. While some reporters, most notably ABC News correspondent Sam Donaldson, broke this unwritten ethical code, photo opportunities (usually shortened to photo ops) became a standard tool of the Reagan White House. Clearly, the photo op did much to further diminish the role of substance in the policy-making process, since correspondents could not ask the president questions about the policy implications of the appearances.

There is a reason why Reagan was so effective in handling the press. He had "arrived in the White House with a strategic plan specifically crafted to keep the media at arm's length." The plan was based on a memorandum issued by Professor Robert Entman of Duke University. Under this approach, "press conferences were deliberately kept to a minimum, press access to the president was severely restricted, and the press, as a result of the administration manipulation, was practically forced to focus on the content of public policies, rather than the president's political motivations" (G. Rose 1997: 31).

The Reagan administration also followed the Nixon administration's "line of the day." In order to ensure that the media would focus on the White House story rather than a competing story, Reagan's advisers carefully planned the president's schedule so that certain points would be emphasized. Officials were warned not to answer questions about other stories. The president was advised to stay focused on the story of the day. This strategy was extraordinarily successful. More often than not the Reagan White House was able to get the three networks to lead with the story the White House had planned. This led several critics to label the networks as pro-Reagan and as not aggressively pursuing stories critical of the White House. What such criticism overlooks is the innovative techniques used by the Reagan White House to control the news, and its exquisite implementation of these techniques (for more see Speakes with Pack 1988; Fitzwater 1995).

George Bush, Reagan's successor, apparently did not learn or competently apply the tools of his political mentor. The next president, Bill Clinton, however, did. As we have noted, Clinton's presidency did not begin auspiciously. After Clinton had been in office only a few months, Sam Donaldson proclaimed the failure of the Clinton presidency. With the president's approval ratings plummeting into the 30 percent range, few at the time doubted Donaldson's prognosis.

Yet Clinton survived, was reelected to a second term, and at the time this book is being written has approval ratings in the 60 percent range, and this despite the fact of impeachment and the threat of removal from office. What happened? Clearly, Clinton benefited from (1) a sound economy, (2) peace abroad, (3) an unimpressive presidential challenger in Bob Dole, and (4) a perfect political nemesis in then-House Speaker Newt Gingrich. But Clinton and his advisers also made a conscious decision to revisit Ronald Reagan's media playbook. Since early 1995, Clinton was portrayed in settings that emphasized one point: that he was an effective president. Gone were the baggy jogging shorts, the trips to McDonalds, and the impromptu press conferences at which he often verbally stepped on his own message. In their place were visuals of the president standing with police officers, the military, hurricane victims, and foreign leaders, or signing an environmentally friendly executive order at the Grand Canyon. Even while the media aggressively pursued the Monica Lewinsky story, the White House continued to portray the president on the job and apparently unflustered. This was a lesson that the Reagan administration had perfected. They found out that no matter what a particular television correspondent said about the president, if the visuals were positive then the viewer's perception of the president was also likely to be positive. And Clinton's visuals were indeed positive, at least until his televised confession that he had indeed had an improper relationship with Ms. Lewinsky.

Conclusions

We are now in an era of new communication technologies, some of which will have an impact on how the president relates to the press and the public. Already, the "Net" or the "Web" has become the source of information from the White House, Congress, and other federal agencies, as well as rumor, gossip, and some hard news from various private organizations. As new technologies develop, it is our hypothesis that public expectations of the president will continue to change. In other words, public expectations seem to be strongly connected to the manner in which presidents communicate with the public. Expectations shifted dramatically as we moved from an era in which newspapers were the primary source of political information to one in which radio and television are the dominant vehicles for political communication.

Throughout the nineteenth century, presidents were remote figures in American political life, largely detached from the mass of citizens. Their political messages and public images were filtered and shaped by intermediary agents, the press and the political parties. The American public did not expect the president to be the national leader, but rather they saw him as the executor of the laws and a check on the excesses of Congress. The public's perception of the president was that of Chief Magistrate, not its Commander-in-Chief.

But the broadcast technologies of radio and television have made political communication direct, instantaneous, and visual. The media's insatiable desire (or need) for new, simple (or sensational) stories with eye-catching pictures has shifted the news reporter's attention to the president from the multiple actors, complex squabbles, and arcane maneuvering in Congress. The public now see and hear the president directly and therefore form their own perceptions of his or her personality, ability, and effectiveness. The president is no longer a remote figure, but a person known to every American household with a television set. As a consequence, the public now expects the president to *lead* the nation—to act quickly and decisively in crises, to evoke our best instincts, to assuage our fears, and to simplify the complex. The president is the Commander-in-Chief and should act accordingly. Whether or not the president's performance is perceived to satisfy the public's expectations is largely shaped by the image that is communicated through the media.

As Teddy Roosevelt, Franklin Roosevelt, John Kennedy, and Ronald Reagan have taught us, successful presidents have learned how to use the available communication tools to "connect" with the public and persuasively convey their messages to the public. They took advantage of the new communication technologies and opened new opportunities for their successors to manipulate the media.

These four presidents have provided yet another lesson for future presidents. It is critically important to a presidency's success that the president control his or her public image. The failures in twentieth-century American presidential politics are invariably those presidents who allowed others to shape their images. Lyndon Johnson lost control of his image with the Vietnam War, as did Nixon during the Watergate crisis. Ford, Carter, and Bush never did control their images. Clinton appeared at first to be losing the image game; then he readjusted his techniques for dealing with the media and the public, and in 1995 rose like a phoenix from the political ashes. Future presidents are advised to pay attention to this lesson.

7

....

Where Do We Go
from Here?

What if this is as good as it gets?

— Jack Nicholson, from *As Good as It Gets*

．．

In the first six chapters of this book we first identified and then traced the development of the image-is-everything presidency. We believe it is the central dilemma facing the presidency today, because it puts the public relation's cart before the policy horse. The end result is an image-driven presidency in which policies often serve as mere props for presidents and their image makers. Substance has been devalued and replaced with symbolism and style. In this process, reality has become confused with the world of the image maker.

In this chapter we ask some basic questions: Where do we go from here? How can we bring substance back into the presidency, and can it be done? To answer these questions we will first revisit some major themes that run through the book.

Public Expectations and Constitutional Authority

Richard Waterman has written, "A dominant theme of the presidential literature is that there is a gap between what the public expects and what presidents can actually accomplish" (1993: 23). Public expectations are particularly important in our governmental system because our constitution does not clearly articulate the parameters of presidential power. While our Founding Fathers had a clear sense of what the legislative branch would look like, they had no such picture of the executive branch. Writing to George Washington on April 16, 1787, just prior to the Constitutional Convention, James Madison—the author of the Virginia Plan—stated, "I have scarcely ventured as yet to form my own opinion either of the manner in which [the executive] ought to be constituted or of the authorities with which it ought to be cloathed" (quoted in Thach, 1969: 83). Few other delegates to the constitutional convention had a clear sense of how the executive branch should be constituted either. It is thus not surprising that most of what was written about the presidency in Article II of the Constitution does not deal with the president's powers and responsibilities.

An analysis of the content of Article II of the Constitution indicates that the Founding Fathers' major concern was *selecting* the president. Table 7.1 shows that fully 46 percent of the words in this article describe the various procedures and qualifications for selecting a president; 8 percent are related to presidential succession; 3 percent to impeachment; and 4.7 percent to compensation. These factors account for almost 62 percent of the words in Article II. In contrast, only 38 percent deal with the actual enumerated powers of the presidency. An examination of the number of words in Article II, however, is only a very rough indicator. Clearly, extraordinary powers can be delegated in only a few words, such as, the president is "Commander-in-Chief of the Army and Navy . . ." Still, especially if we examine the detailed explication of the powers of the legislative branch in Article I of the Constitution, our analysis of Article II suggests that the Founding Fathers indeed did not have a clear idea of precisely what they wanted the presidency to be.

An examination of the constitutional debate in 1787 provides further evidence on this point. Little of the debate was related to the prospective powers of the presidency. Mostly, the Founders dealt with (1) whether the nation should have a plural or single chief executive and (2) the method that should be used for selecting the president. According to constitutional expert Charles Thach, as the end of July approached "the truth is that, while the Convention thought itself ready to proceed to the business of drawing up a draft of a constitution on the basis of the

. . . .

TABLE 7.1

Content Analysis of Article II of the Constitution

Provision	Words	Percentage
Executive vesting clause	15	1.5
Election of president	463	46.0
Succession	83	8.0
Compensation	48	4.7
Oath of office	54	5.3
Commander-in-chief	34	3.4
Opinion of department heads	28	2.8
Pardons and reprieves	21	2.0
Treaties	25	2.5
Appointments	115	19.5
State of the Union	31	3.0
Convene congress	38	3.7
Receive ambassadors	8	0.7
Laws faithfully executed	20	2.0
Impeachment	31	3.0

general principles, so far as the executive was concerned they had settled practically nothing except the question of unity and the veto power" (1969: 103–104). Nor was there much debate about presidential power during August. As Donald Robinson wrote, "During the month of August, when so much time was spent devising the electoral scheme, there was little attention given to the question of presidential powers" (1987: 89). As a result, Thach has commented:

> The completion of Article II of the Constitution seems, at first sight, a logical place for an evaluation of the work of the Convention and an interpretation of the executive established by it. A closer view reveals the fact that such an evaluation and interpretation is hardly possible. Rushed through in the last days of the Convention's being, as much of it was, the executive article fairly bristles with contentious matter, and, until it is seen what decision was given to these contentions, it is impossible to say just what the national executive meant. (1969: 140)

Because the power of the presidency was not clearly articulated in the Constitution, public expectations of presidential performance have become of particular importance. As Barbara Hinckley wrote, "In an office left undefined, public expectations can be critically important" (1985: 22). She later elaborated on this point, stating that the "office is undefined; thus presidents become what people want them to be." In this process "[e]xpectations shape action; action leads to further expectations" (Hinckley 1990: 8–9).

As noted in Chapter 1, today, most presidential scholars believe that the public has excessive and even unrealistic expectations of the presidency. But, as we argued in Chapter 2, public expectations are not static. In fact, they have changed radically over time. For example, early in our nation's history the public did not expect its presidents to be (1) politically ambitious, (2) to actively promote a legislative agenda, or (3) to speak or campaign publicly, in other words, to be particularly active in the governmental process. While presidents could be active in foreign affairs, our nineteenth-century presidents had relatively little opportunity in this policy realm. In accord with such expectations, most of these presidents did not govern actively and those few who did were generally denounced as being tyrants or kings. On the other hand, the public did expect its nineteenth-century presidents to be common men who exhibited high levels of honesty and virtue. As a result of such public expectations, then, presidents, on the whole, tended to (1) disavow political ambition (at least publicly), (2) seldom speak in public, (3) not campaign for office, (4) most often defer to Congress on domestic policy matters, and (5) associated themselves with common man symbols such as log cabins and rail splitting. Public expectations, then, did much to shape the comportment of our nineteenth-century presidents.

By the turn of the twentieth century, however, public expectations were begin-ning to change. Industrialization and the beginning of an exodus of the rural population to the cities was placing greater demands on government at all levels. Concomitantly, America was taking its first tenuous steps onto the world stage. At the same time, a national press corps was developing that provided presidents a greater opportunity to be seen and heard directly by the public. In this changing political environment, Teddy Roosevelt brought a new sense of vigor and activity to the White House. Not only did he articulate a broader interpretation of the Constitution, he also energized the presidency. The public was enthralled with its new young president, and Roosevelt took full advantage of the increased public and press interest to move the presidency toward the fulcrum of our governmen-tal system. While he did not complete this process, he did more than any presi-dent since George Washington to influence what the public expected from its presidents. After Teddy Roosevelt, it would be difficult for presidents to go back to the bland nineteenth-century model of the presidency.

Franklin Roosevelt (FDR) completed what Teddy Roosevelt had begun, a verita-ble revolution in public perceptions of the presidency. During FDR's 12-plus years in the White House, the public came to look to Washington, and more impor-tantly to the presidency, for solutions to all sorts of problems. FDR willingly en-couraged the public to shift its attention and its expectations toward the presi-dency. It was through this process that the modern presidency was established, presidential power was exponentially increased, and the president became the cen-tral focus in our governmental system. Over time, however, the public came to ex-pect too much from its presidents: a sound economy, a good job, peace abroad, housing for the poor, health care for all, and so on. As a result, by the 1960s, presi-dential scholars were noting with alarm that the public actually expected *too much* from its presidents, and that these excessive expectations were threatening the presidency. They warned that a series of failed presidencies would be the result.

While empirical work has demonstrated that the gap exists and that it does in-deed have a deleterious impact on presidential performance (Stimson 1976; 1976-1977; Raichur and Waterman 1993; Waterman, Jenkins-Smith, and Silva Forth-coming), one point that we can derive from this book is that there is no reason to believe that this state of affairs will be permanent. In fact, we have shown that ex-pectations are highly mutable.

There is already some indication that public expectations may be changing. As our country's presidents have faced one personal crisis after another (for example, Watergate, Iran-Contra, Whitewater, campaign-finance abuse, and the Monica Lewinsky affair), the public may be beginning to expect less of its presidents. As noted in Chapter 3, a public realization that Bill Clinton was a womanizer and that he shaded the truth ironically appears to have lowered expectations about Clinton's performance. People were therefore not surprised when Clinton was charged with improprieties involving campaign financing in the White House or sexual relations with a White House intern. But the same public held Vice President Al Gore—who had an impeccable reputation—to a much higher standard in the campaign-financing scandal.

The Monica Lewinsky case, discussed in Chapter 6, is particularly instructive in this regard. In January 1998, allegations first surfaced that President Bill Clinton had had sexual relations with a White House intern named Monica Lewinsky. It was also alleged that he had perjured himself in testimony in the Paula Jones civil suit, a case brought against Clinton in which he was accused of blatant sexual harassment of Ms. Jones when he was governor of Arkansas. Allegations also surfaced that President Clinton had suborned perjury by trying to convince Ms. Lewinsky to deny that she had had sex with him and that he had obstructed justice by telling Ms. Lewinsky not to turn over various gifts he had given her and which were then subpoenaed by Paula Jones' attorneys. If true, these allegations represented potentially impeachable offenses. After all, it was a charge of obstruction of justice that had forced Richard Nixon to resign from office. Even beyond the legal charges, the allegations of sex in the Oval Office were certainly seamy and not in accord with what scholars contended the public expects from its presidents—for example, high moral standards.

What then was the public response to these allegations? In a February 1998 CBS News/*New York Times* poll, 68 percent of the respondents said they approved of Bill Clinton's job performance (*New York Times*, 2–24–98: A1 and A14). At the same time, 59 percent said they were "inclined to believe that President Clinton had an affair with Monica S. Lewinsky." Another 59 percent also said they "would understand if Clinton were not telling the truth about his sexual conduct." Concomitantly, however, 55 percent said the president had "a responsibility to be completely truthful when questioned in public about his sex life." As political pundits routinely predicted the end of the Clinton presidency, only 21 percent of the respondents believed the president should "resign," and only 12 percent favored his impeachment; 46 percent felt an apology would be sufficient, while 16 percent believed the whole matter should be dropped. Clearly, if the public had inflated expectations of presidential performance, the poll results should have indicated greater dissatisfaction with Clinton's presidency.

The poll results were not transitory, either. Clinton's approval ratings continued in the 60 percent range throughout the spring of 1998 and throughout the rest of the year, reaching at times nearly 70 percent! For instance, just prior to

Clinton's August 17th testimony before a grand jury and his televised admission that night that he had indeed had an improper relationship with Ms. Lewinsky, 55 percent of the respondents to a *Newsweek* (8–24–98: 22–23) poll (conducted on August 13–14, 1998) said that Bill Clinton did not have "the honesty and integrity they expect in a president." Yet, in the very same poll, by a margin of 53 to 21 percent, respondents said that "a president's effectiveness in carrying out policies beneficial to the country matters more than high personal character." The president's job approval rating in that poll was 59 percent.

Following the president's public speech, which many newspaper editorialists—including the *New York Times* and the *Washington Post*—characterized as inadequate and even self-serving, on the ABC News program *Nightline* (8–19–98), Ted Koppel revealed that in an ABC News poll the president's approval rating remained firm at 60 percent. In addition, more than 60 percent of the public did not want the president to resign or to be impeached. On the other hand, the president's unfavorability rating soared, and solid majorities displayed increasing displeasure with the president's personal comportment. It should be noted, however, that this poll was conducted after Clinton's confession but before the U.S. Tomahawk cruise missile attack on August 20 on targets in the Sudan and Afghanistan in retaliation for the terrorist bombing of U.S. embassies in Kenya and Tanzania. As political pundits continued to discuss the possibilities of a presidential impeachment or resignation, the public continued to express its solid approval for the president's job performance, though the slide in his personal favorability ratings still showed a considerable erosion of support.

While these poll results clearly expressed satisfaction with such other factors as the state of the nation's economy and the fact that the nation was at peace, this reaction was far different from the one in the case of the Iran-Contra affair just twelve years before. In 1986, when it was alleged that President Ronald Reagan had indeed traded arms for hostages, his approval ratings plummeted—one of the largest drops in presidential approval ratings ever measured by the Gallup polling organization. There are clear similarities between the two cases. In 1986, as in 1998, the country was generally prosperous and at peace. Reagan, like Clinton, was also a second-term president who could not run for office again and would leave office voluntarily in about two years. The difference is that Reagan's actions involved his official presidential duties, while the public interpreted Clinton's behavior as largely a private matter. Still, based on the theory that the public has excessive and unrealistic expectations of presidential performance, we would have expected a much harsher public reaction to the initial charges that Bill Clinton had had an affair with Ms. Lewinsky and then later to his publicly televised confession, watched by an estimated 67 million Americans. That the public continued to approve of Clinton's job performance while it had turned overwhelmingly—if only temporarily—against Reagan is evidence that the public was once again beginning to alter its expectations of the presidency by the end of the twentieth century.

How then can we explain the Clinton-Lewinsky case? Is it indeed evidence that the public expects less from its presidents? Media and public opinion expert John Zaller (1998: 184) examined a series of public opinion polls following the initial allegation that Clinton had had sex with the young intern. He finds that initially the president's "support fell about 7 percentage points." During this period "media coverage was sharply negative." Clinton then publicly denied having had "sex with that woman, Monica Lewinsky." The first lady, Hillary Rodham Clinton, on NBC's *Today Show,* then claimed that this was all a right-wing conspiracy. As the president and first lady issued their denials, media coverage of the president became more balanced and Clinton "gained back those 7 points and added an additional 8 to 10 points of support." In other words, the public did react negatively to the initial charge, but also responded to the first couple's denials and to the president's State of the Union address, in which he appeared to be calm and in control. And while the president's approval ratings following his televised confession did not change much (in some polls his approval ratings actually increased slightly), his personal favorability ratings plummeted, as they had in January 1998. In sum, there is some evidence that the public was dissatisfied with Bill Clinton in January and August 1998. Still, the negative public reaction was not nearly as severe in either case as was the reaction to the news that Reagan had traded arms for hostages in 1986.

Beyond the specific case of the Clinton-Lewinsky situation, there is additional evidence that public expectations may be changing. Regarding the performance of presidents in general, in the February 1998 CBS News/*New York Times* poll, 84 percent of the respondents agreed that "someone can be a good President even if they do things in their personal life that you disapprove of" (*New York Times,* 2-24-98: A1 and A14). Furthermore, in a November 1992 Gallup poll, while most people expected newly elected President Bill Clinton to be an "outstanding" or "above average" president, over 70 percent "did not expect him to keep his campaign promise not to raise taxes, and clear majorities did not expect him to reduce the deficit or control federal spending" (Edwards and Wayne 1997: 100). If expectations are in fact changing (and we will need more evidence than simply evaluations of one president to judge whether the public really expects less from its presidents in general), then this will likely have an impact on how presidents are elected and how they govern.

The main point to remember, though, is that public expectations are not fixed and immutable. They can and have changed over time, and the changes have had a major impact on how the presidency has evolved. And with changes in public expectations we have concomitantly witnessed changes in the images presidents have employed.

Historical Images

Changes in public expectations also have been associated with changes in historical images over time. As noted in Chapter 2, the common man image was relevant to the public expectations of the late nineteenth century. The public did not expect its presidents to be politically ambitious, nor was the presidency an activist institution. Thus, many presidents of this era successfully associated themselves with such symbols as log cabins in order to demonstrate that they were common men. But, as public expectations changed and the public began to expect more from its presidents, the common man image ultimately became a political liability. (Such modern-era presidents as Harry Truman, Gerald Ford, and Jimmy Carter found that they were considered too common and not big enough to be president.) Clearly, then, as public expectations changed, a new historical image of the presidency would be required.

The new image of president as master politician began to prevail. As the public turned its attention toward Washington and the White House, presidents started associating themselves with activist images. They traveled and spoke more often. Since a master politician had to accomplish more of substance, this historical image clearly promoted substantive achievements. Teddy Roosevelt thus could tout the "Square Deal," Woodrow Wilson the "New Freedom," FDR the "New Deal," Harry Truman the "Fair Deal," John Kennedy the "New Frontier," and Lyndon Johnson the "Great Society." This era saw the enactment of landmark legislation involving almost every facet of American life.

The world of 1932, the year Franklin Roosevelt was first elected, was vastly different from the world of Richard Nixon, 1974, when the last of the master politician presidents left the scene. Much of this change can be attributed to the policy activism of these presidents. But such activism encouraged further changes in public expectations. By the end of this era, scholars were noting with increasing concern that the public had come to expect too much from its presidents. And the presidents had clearly encouraged this trend by promising too much, often more than they could reasonably be expected to deliver. A gap therefore developed between what the public expected and what presidents could actually accomplish. As the expectations gap widened, presidents found public expectations to be an enemy they needed to conquer rather than an ally in the political wars with Congress. As presidents found themselves incapable of following through on all of their promises, they came to be seen in a new light by the public: mere politicians—in the most negative sense of the word—willing to say and do whatever was necessary to get elected. Lying and dishonesty became unwanted parts of the image associated with the last of the master politician presidents. Following the failed presidencies of Lyndon Johnson and Richard Nixon, then, presidents found it necessary to turn to yet a new historical image in an attempt to ameliorate public expectations.

The current historical image presidents use to govern is the Washington outsider image. Presidents and presidential contenders have tried to distance themselves from the master politician image by casting verbal charges at the Washington establishment—even if they have been intimately involved in Washington politics. They have tried to associate themselves with the best part of the common man image—they are again more like us than they are like a traditional politician. But they do not portray themselves as too common and thus not capable of being president. Instead, Washington outsiders claim to have the experience to be leaders, but, in a somewhat contradictory fashion, they wallow in their lack of Washington experience. What they invoke are images of bedrock American values: home and hearth.

The Washington outsider image has two basic problems: (1) presidents, once elected, are unlikely to be able to work with the Washington establishment (which they attacked throughout the campaign), and (2) presidents are less likely to have the necessary Washington-level experience to be capable of governing effectively once they are elected. Hence, this image gets the president elected, but it does little to equip him or her for the task of governing in Washington. Consequently, it is not particularly well suited to satisfying public expectations, at least not with substantive achievements. As a result, presidents have found it necessary to create personal images that present them in a positive light before the American public (see Chapter 3). The result is an image-driven presidency, one in which images are transitory and disposable.

The Image-Is-Everything Presidency

Along with the growth of the Washington outsider image, we have identified what we believe to be a disturbing development in the evolution of the presidency: the creation of the Image-Is-Everything Presidency. Images have always been important to the presidency. In his delineation of the so-called "hats" that presidents wear (a symbol for the major responsibilities of the presidency), historian Clinton

Rossiter (1960) identified the presidential role of "Chief of State." This role is largely symbolic and can be equated with the role of the king or queen of England. In this capacity, the president is the symbol of our nation. When presidents attend a myriad of public events (for example, funerals of foreign dignitaries), they do so as the Chief of State. Images and symbols are therefore built into the very job description of the presidency. Likewise, historical images of presidents and the presidency have evolved over time. And we have argued that many presidents carefully chose symbols that would best represent them to the nation at particular periods in American history. We furthermore argued that some historical images are more conducive to a particular historical time than others.

While image making has always been important to the presidency, then, the image making of the image-is-everything presidency has become preeminent among our most recent cohort of presidents. Certainly, image has often—though we acknowledge not always (1981 and the Reagan Revolution is a good counterexample)—become more important than policy substance.

There is, we believe, a method to this madness. Our most recent presidents, who are aware that many of their predecessors have failed in their attempts to satisfy public expectations, have used polling, focus groups, political consultants, and media experts to craft images that are more acceptable to the American public. As pointed out in Chapter 4, as the political parties have become less and less important and personal political consultants have taken their place in the electoral process, policy substance has become a mere tool for electioneering. Candidates or incumbent presidents run for office by crafting poll- and focus-group-tested images, they provide often cruel caricatures of their political opponents, and they oftentimes try to avoid thorny issues—or even the articulation of a clear policy agenda—all in order to better advance their electoral prospects. While favorable personal images are often created—for example, this president will be tough on crime and national defense and will stand up to the big-spending liberals in Congress—the image-is-everything president does not have a useful basis for governing. As we pointed out in Chapter 4, since 1968 in only one election was a clear policy agenda articulated, Ronald Reagan's 1980 campaign. Mostly, presidential candidates have spouted platitudes about the issues, for example, Gary Hart's mantra in the 1984 Democratic primary season—he stood for "New Ideas." What these new ideas were we never found out. Hart's Democratic challenger in the 1984 primaries, Walter Mondale, questioned Hart about the content of his new ideas. In a presidential debate Mondale asked, "Where's the beef?," using a line from a popular hamburger commercial to tell the American public that there was no substance to Hart's ideas. But Mondale did not take this opportunity to tell us what *his* ideas were. After all, ideas and policy substance were not as important as scoring political points. The idea was to show that your opponent did not have any ideas, not that you did.

Presidents today often identify themselves with issues over which they ultimately will have little influence as president. For instance, presidents are quick to say they are for education or tough on crime, leaving the public to remember that these issues are largely local and state governmental responsibilities. Presidents can pass a crime bill or ask for more federal money for education, but that is basically the limit of their influence.

Like the Washington outsider image, then, the image-is-everything presidency does not have a solid basis for sound governance once the elections are over. Instead, presidents such as Bill Clinton have found it easier to continue the campaign, essentially running for a second term from their very first day in office; this constant campaigning means there is even less time for governance. In summary, the image-is-everything presidency crowds out policy substance, subverting it by making it a prop for image making and reducing it to mere empty rhetoric that may sound good but cannot be easily translated into policy.

As pointed out in Chapter 5, once presidents are elected, they speak more often, but they are not doing so in settings that are particularly conducive to informing the nation about substantive issues. They are more likely to speak at ceremonial or political events, in front of specialized audiences. Even when they address the nation as a whole in major speeches, presidents are still likely to invoke symbols and to present a highly unrealistic portrayal of the president's powers and responsibilities. As presidents speak more and more often, policy substance seems to be even less on their minds and appears less in their speeches. Furthermore, the more they speak the less time they actually have to govern.

Finally, in Chapter 6 we argued that, ironically, the media has also played an important role in the development of the image-is-everything presidency. Sound-bite journalism and an emphasis on visuals and soft news over an analysis of the issues has given presidents an incentive to manipulate the media for their own advantage. Presidents and their advisers thus spend more time on the setting for a president's speech than on what the president will say. They pay more attention to the potential sound bites in the speech than to whether the speech as a whole conveys a coherent or consistent meaning.

The view of the presidency that we have delineated throughout this book is not a rosy one. There are indeed serious problems with the state of the presidency as we come to the end of the twentieth century and get ready to embark upon a new millennium. While we do not believe the presidency is doomed or that all presidents must necessarily fail, and while individual presidents, at least for short periods of time, have shown an ability to achieve substantive policy accomplishments (for example, Reagan in 1981 and 1982, Clinton in 1993 and 1996), the recent image-is-everything presidencies raise serious questions about the relationship between substance and governing. Can something be done about it?

"What If This Is as Good as It Gets?"

Before we can answer the question of whether anything can be done to ameliorate the negative effects of the image-is-everything presidency, we need to recognize that the process we have described in this book has been an evolutionary one. We emphasized an historical approach to the study of image making to show how closely image making is tied to public expectations and how these expectations have changed radically over time. In an era in which the public had only limited expectations of presidential performance, it was rational for presidents to adopt images that (1) eschewed political ambition and (2) portrayed them as common men. Likewise, as the public came to expect more from the federal government and its presidents, it was rational for presidents to (1) adopt action-oriented images, (2) seize the center of the domestic political stage, (3) become a major player on the world stage, and (4) promise the public ever more accomplishments, even if these promises at times ultimately proved to be unreasonable.

In the present age, "going public" is a more useful strategy than backroom bargaining and persuasion. It is an age of a cynical media and of a public with an anti-Washington bias, and one in which television has emerged as the dominant means of communication between presidents and the public. Presidents and presidential candidates have quite naturally shifted ground once again. With the term *politician* taking on a highly negative connotation, today's presidents and presidential candidates have adopted images that stress (1) that they are not traditional politicians and (2) that they are not really members of the Washington establishment, even if they really have been for many years (for example, Bob Dole in the 1996 presidential campaign—he had been in Congress since the 1960s). We believe, however, that it is not useful for us to berate the individuals who have adopted these images, because recent history demonstrates that these images work. Jimmy Carter, Ronald Reagan, and Bill Clinton rode to the White House on the image of the Washington outsider. Numerous other presidential candidates likely got more attention than they otherwise would have by adopting the image (Lamar Alexander, for example). The Republicans regained control of the House of Representatives and the Senate in 1994 by portraying the long-entrenched Democratic establishment as traditional politicians, voicing strident anti-Washington themes, and running outsider candidates.

Likewise, we can lament the formation of the image-is-everything presidency, but, again, it has served the interests of many politicians well. While George Bush's "read my lips" pledge was clearly a disastrous use of image creation, Ronald Reagan much more successfully crafted an image of toughness to get him elected: a cowboy on a horse, the ultimate outsider. And even if Bill Clinton's "building a bridge to the twenty-first century" rhetoric from the 1996 presidential campaign was largely devoid of any real content, it did help Clinton to win a second term in the White House. While we can criticize its lack of substance and state the obvious, that it left Clinton with no policy mandate for his second term, his public relations team can respond with: So what, it got him reelected, didn't it? For Clinton and other recent presidents, then, the establishment of the image-is-everything presidency is not a fact to be lamented, but an opportunity to use ever newer political technologies to secure election and reelection. Clearly, for some, then, image making has paid big dividends.

Hence, while we argue that the policy horse needs to be put back in front of the public relations cart, we are coming from a somewhat different direction than the practitioners who benefit from these new image making strategies and approaches. We contend that this most recent evolution in the presidency has perniciously devalued policy substance, which often becomes a mere prop for image making. They can contend that the Washington outsider image and the image-is-everything presidency have been extraordinarily useful in electing a number of candidates to office. From the perspective of the image maker and the politician, then, this book might have been better titled *Much Ado About Nothing*. For to them, the process is working as planned—that is, they are getting elected. The sad reality is that we are both probably right.

But we have not written this book from the perspective of the individual politician. As academics we are looking at the bigger picture. Our interest is in the effect these images have on the way our governmental system operates. In that sense we are extremely concerned. Democracy cannot function properly if image is everything. The world of the image maker and the pseudo-event can give us the happy impression that things are indeed better and that we are better off, when in fact nothing much of substance has really been accomplished. **Substance is important, even if it doesn't always win elections.**

The problem, as we see it, is that so long as the Washington outsider and image-is-everything presidency approaches serve the electoral interests of candidates, they will not abandon them. We are sure that Ronald Reagan in 1984 or Bill Clinton in 1996 would rather have been reelected without a clear policy mandate than to have suffered the fate of Jimmy Carter in 1980 or George Bush in 1992. Hence, while we can recommend changes in the current system, there is a built-in incentive for politicians to continue to use these images. That is, until public expectations change again and the images are no longer useful. If past history is any indication, we can assert with considerable certainty that the current historical and personal images will at some future time no longer be useful. We cannot predict how they will change, but as public expectations of the political system inevitably shift, the images that presidents adopt will change also. What is difficult to determine is whether the new images will be more substantive or even less so. Although for the foreseeable future the Washington outsider and image-is-everything presidency should predominate, we have to remember, as pointed out earlier, that the public relations cart has not always been in front of the policy horse. The master politician image, while it had many negative attributes (for example, it encouraged politicians to promise too much and fostered a Machiavellian leadership approach), was the most "policy-substantive" of the three historical images we described. In fact, a record of substantive achievement was critical to this image. Consequently, new images may yet be created that again encourage more substantive policy debate and accomplishment. We do not see them on the political horizon at present, however.

Given the evolutionary nature of presidential image making, then, what can be done to address the central dilemma of the presidency today? Our recommendations are not new, and we are not particularly optimistic that they can all be adopted, but it is better than telling our readers: just wait for a new historical image. Our first recommendation pertains to the media. As we argued in Chapters 5 and 6, television clearly plays a critical role in the image-is-everything presidency. Television emphasizes visuals over substantive speech, sound bites over deliberation, and pseudo-events over hard political news. To ameliorate these tendencies, we recommend that the news media provide presidents and presidential candidates free TV time to address the nation, perhaps in five-minute increments, but only if they agree to (1) address a substantive issue and (2) not mention their opponent, except in terms of their opponent's view on the issue. In sum, these forums should be specifically designed to allow the candidate to tell the nation what he or she will do once elected.

Second, the cost and length of presidential campaigns need to be lessened and shortened, respectively. One important step would be the enactment of serious campaign-finance reform legislation. The present system, which allows veritably unlimited use of "soft money" in campaigns, has provided the president with yet another "hat" (to use Clinton Rossiter's (1960) metaphor): Chief Campaign-Fund-Raiser. Presidents are regularly asked to raise money, not only for their own campaign, but also for House, Senate, and state-level candidates. As a result, Bill Clinton, for example, held various fund-raising events right in the White House prior to the 1996 presidential election. In addition, Clinton and Vice President Al Gore were accused of soliciting funds directly from within the White House, including making potentially illegal calls from White House phones. Beyond the questionable ethics and legality of these actions, presidents cannot do the business of the country if they are constantly forced to appear at fund-raisers and other campaign events. Making the president the Chief Campaign-Fund-Raiser imperils the integrity of the office. For example, in 1996 the specter of campaign contributions emanating from the Chinese government raised fundamental questions about the influence fund-raising may have on our nation's foreign policy. If substantive promises are made to other nations in order to secure campaign funds, then policy substance is being even more seriously subverted than we have alleged throughout this book.

Regarding the length of campaigns, a number of proposals designed to shorten the primary season have been advanced. Some pundits have called for a national primary or a series of national primaries (see G. Rose 1997).

While these changes may prove beneficial in shortening the campaign, a possible disadvantage is that they also could make it virtually impossible for lesser known candidates to have a serious chance of securing the nomination. It certainly would give candidates capable of raising large sums of money a major advantage, thus possibly undoing any benefit that would derive from campaign-finance reform. Hence, while we support in theory the idea of shortening the campaign season, we are not yet convinced that any of the existing proposals would not produce unintended and unwanted political costs. Clearly, shortening the campaign season will not be an easy task.

Third, the media needs to be more responsible in covering the presidency. Wild speculation and sensationalism need to be balanced with informing the public about the substance of policy. Why not assign five minutes on network newscasts to an informative discussion of a relevant substantive issue (for example, the budget, health care, and so on)? There has been some progress on this front: CBS's *Eye on America*, as well as similar features on NBC and ABC newscasts. We encourage the networks to expand these features and develop new ones. Clearly, although focusing on sex scandals or sensational events such as the O. J. Simpson murder trial or the death of Princess Diana provides hefty ratings for the network news broadcasts, the networks and our nation's newspapers also have a responsibility to inform the public of more substantive news. Cotton candy journalism may sell newspapers or secure viewers, but it does not inform the public about the substance of important issues. As we argued in Chapter 6, the television news programs have provided the incentive for sound-bite journalism and the predominance of visuals, which means that they can change the dynamics of how the news is reported. They can provide more time for candidates to speak, as with the five-minute proposal we advanced above. They can also inform the public about the role of visuals and images in American politics. Have you, for example, ever wondered why, when the president of the United States addresses the nation from his desk in the Oval Office, the pictures on his desk—usually of his wife and family—are turned toward the camera and not toward himself? When most of us put pictures on our desks we place them so that we can look at them, not so that others coming into the room can see them. Placing the pictures facing the camera subliminally shows us that the president is indeed a good family man. It is a subtle use of image making, one that often goes overlooked by the media. We believe the media need to be more attentive to identifying this type of image making. Perhaps specific reporters could be assigned to what could be called **the image desk,** to focus on the subject of image politics. Uncovering how these images are created and used could be both entertaining and informative.

Obviously, in offering these recommendations, we do not put all of the blame for the declining role of substance in American politics on presidents, their advisers, the campaign process, or the media. We the public have to share the blame. While TV news and newspapers have become more concerned with sensational stories and have thus often moved substance off the front page, we live in a society in which information is omnipresent. We may have to be a bit more diligent in searching for it, but the information is already there. For example, the discriminating viewer can turn to C-SPAN or to in-depth newscasts on PBS for a more nuanced and detailed examination of the news. Clearly, many viewers already do, but not nearly a majority of us. There also are substantive publications (both newspapers and magazines), as well as a plethora of information on the World Wide Web. Hence, while the influence of television on the presidency has certainly been pernicious, it alone cannot be blamed for all of the presidency's problems. Clearly, as stated above, some of the blame rests with ourselves. Sadly, for many of us (even those of us writing this book), there is a fascination with the pseudo-event and the tools of the image makers. It is too easy to forget the substance of politics. Be honest, how many of you would rather watch a *Nightline* program on the president's latest sex scandal than a program on the details of the latest presidential budget proposal? All of us should hold government and politics to a higher standard. We should also expect less of our governmental leaders. But will we? At the risk of being characterized as pessimists, our answer is: probably not. Sensationalism, image, and style will generally triumph over substance. Image is everything in large part because we are attracted to images.

Hence, presidents are indeed rational actors. They understand the nature of the game as it played today. A president who is not concerned with his or her image is likely to be perceived as naive and, ultimately, a failure. Presidents who do not play to the television screen will likely be one-term presidents. Presidents who do not listen to their pollsters, political consultants, and public relations teams will later be excoriated by history as foolish or naive. Rational presidents (and other rational members of the Washington community) know what the parameters and rules of the political game are. Unless some new technology evolves that changes those rules, or unless television suddenly becomes more responsible or the public more inquisitive (both of which we doubt), politicians will continue to rely on their public relations operations, both in running for president and in governing the nation. Simply stated, it is rational for them to do so.

The media are also rational actors. As long as they are rewarded with high ratings and profitable subscription rates for doing so, they will continue to cover these pseudo-events. Pseudo-events may make for poor presidential leadership, but they certainly make for great television; and that, sad to say, is all that much of the media is interested in. Great visuals will beat detail and nuance every single time. In fact, the less complicated the story is, the better it usually plays on television.

If presidents and the media are thus both responding to the present political environment in rational ways, there is little likelihood that the system will change anytime soon. In short, we can think of no magical solution to the image-is-everything presidency. Some stimulus is required to change the present political equation, probably a new interactive technology. Until then, our expectation is that the image-is-everything presidency will continue to develop and thrive; image will be everything.

Discussion Questions

Chapter 1

1. As you read your local newspaper, pay particular attention for a couple of days to stories about the president. What types of events does he or she participate in during this period of time? Can the events be classified as pseudo-events? Why or why not?

2. Do you think the public expects too much of its presidents? Explain your answer.

3. Read a book about your favorite president. Make a list of the images associated with that president. What do those images tell you about him or her?

Chapter 2

1. What are the similarities and differences between the three historical images identified in this chapter?

2. Can presidents adopt more than one historical image at a time?

3. How are the historical images identified in this chapter related to the public's expectations of presidential performance?

Chapter 3

1. When you think of the president, which images come immediately to your mind? List three to five. What do the images tell you about the president?

2. Name some personal images that you believe all presidents wish to be associated with. Why are these particular personal images important?

3. Name some personal images that presidents do not wish to be associated with. What is the problem with these personal images?

Chapter 4

1. The example of the 1920 presidential election shows that the emphasis on image over substance is not new to presidential politics. What are some of the similarities and differences between the way presidential images were "handled" then and how they're handled now? Could a candidate such as Warren Harding be nominated today? Why or why not?

2. Much has been made in recent times about the vast sums of money that presidential campaigns must raise in order for candidates to be competitive in elections. How has the rising cost of presidential campaigns affected the length and cost of these campaigns?

3. We have made the argument that the emphasis on images for the sake of campaigns has come at a cost to effective governing. What are the crucial differences between campaigning and governing? Is it possible for governance to be separated from campaign images?

Chapter 5

1. Log on to the White House web site (at www.WhiteHouse.gov) on the Internet or examine the *Public Papers of the President*. Read two or three speeches dealing with a policy that you are particularly interested in, such as the environment, crime, or education. Are there substantive proposals in these speeches or is their content largely symbolic?

2. Watch the president deliver a speech on C-SPAN, where you will see the complete presidential address. Describe the nature of the president's remarks and the audience for which it is intended. Is the president speaking to the nation or to a specific group?

3. Presidential experts often claim that only individuals who look good on television or who speak well can be effective presidents today. Do you agree or disagree with this statement? Do you think that speechmaking should play a central role in the presidency?

Chapter 6

1. Do the media simply report the news or do they interpret it as well? What are the implications of the way news about presidents and presidential candidates is reported?

2. How have technological developments altered the way in which the media report on political actors and political events? How do you think the Internet and other evolving technologies will change the way the media report the news in the future?

3. Watch the news coverage of the president on television for one week. In which settings is the president portrayed? Is the media coverage of the president factual, objective, or biased?

Chapter 7

1. In this chapter we offered several recommendations for dealing with the image-is-everything presidency. What other changes or reforms could make our political system more substantive?

2. We argue that the image-is-everything presidency is a serious problem facing the nation. Do you agree, or do you believe that it represents a lesser threat to American politics? If so, why?

3. Do you think that the American public holds some responsibility for the rise of image politics? Should the public be more knowledgeable about its politicians' statements, policies, and activities?

Glossary

Common Man Image   An historical image in which presidents and presidential candidates portray themselves as "one of us," a typical American. This image has become less useful since the advent of the modern presidency.

Expectations Gap   The gap between what the public expects from its presidents and what presidents can actually do.

Historical Images   Broad presidential images that reoccur over time and generally reflect the prevailing attitudes or expectations of a particular era or period in American history.

Image Desk   Our recommendation in which reporters would focus on the subject of image politics. They would examine how presidents and other politicians use images in elections and the governance process.

Image-Is-Everything Presidency   The presidency in which carefully constructed, poll-tested images defined presidents, elevated the importance of public relations, and devalued the importance of policy substance.

Independent Journalism   The nonpartisan, objective reporting that became the professional ethic in the twentieth century, in contrast to the partisan bias of news reporting in the nineteenth century.

Invisible Primaries   Period of time before the beginning of formal primary campaigns when aspiring candidates try to gain the financial and political support needed to run in the primaries. This period usually receives little publicity or media attention.

Iran-Contra Scandal   Scandal involving the Reagan administration. The White House was accused of swapping arms with Iran for American hostages. Then it was revealed that officials from the Reagan administration had sold U.S. equipment to Iran and diverted the funds from these transactions to the contras operating in Nicaragua.

Major Speeches   Speeches such as State of the Union addresses, inaugural addresses, and economic speeches. They are generally delivered in front of a wide audience.

Master Politician Image   An historical image in which presidents assume the posture of an active leader, bargaining and compromising with other Washington insiders. This is the most substantive of the historical images.

Media   The agents of mass communication such as newspapers, magazines, radio, television, and so on.

Minor Speeches   Speeches generally delivered in front of a smaller, more specialized audience.

News Conferences   Situation in which the presidents allow various reporters to ask them questions in an open forum. Since Eisenhower's presidency these conferences have been televised.

Personal Images   Images that individual presidents adopt to look tough on crime, strong on national defense, caring and compassionate, and so on.

Political Consultants   Hired political people who help presidents and other candidates secure political office. In this role they have largely supplanted the political parties. In recent years, they have also played a more active role in setting the president's policy agenda.

Primary Elections   Elections held before the November general election, between January and June, for the purposes of nominating candidates.

Pseudo-Events   Events that are generally staged and geared for political effect. They are often spectacles created for the sole purpose of creating or advancing a presidential image.

Rhetorical Presidency   Scholar Jeffrey Tulis's term to describe the increasing propensity of presidents to lead through speechmaking. This type of presidency was established by Theodore Roosevelt and Woodrow Wilson and has become an integral part of the presidency since Franklin Roosevelt's time.

Sound Bites   Although extended excerpts of presidential speeches used to be shown on the news, only short blips of 6 to 8 seconds are now generally shown. Presidents and other politicians have become adept at making short snappy comments within the speech that can be played within this time frame.

Spin Control   Influencing the way in which the news is reported in order to create the desired interpretation or image.

Washington Outsider Image   An historical image in which presidents portray themselves as apart from the Washington establishment. As a result, they often do not build the necessary connections to govern effectively once they are elected.

Watergate Scandal   Scandal that began when a group of individuals associated with President Nixon's Committee to Re-Elect the President broke into the Democratic National Committee headquarters. Over time, as allegations about the scandal and its related activities became widely disseminated, the impeachment of the president became a real possibility. To forestall this process, Richard Nixon resigned from office in August 1974.

References

Adams, William C. 1987. "As New Hampshire Goes . . ." In Garry Orren and Nelson Polsby (Eds.) *Media and Momentum*. Chatham, N.J.: Chatham House.

Alger, Dean E. 1996. *The Media and Politics*. Belmont: Wadsworth Publishing Company.

Ansolabehere, Stephen, Roy Behr, and Shanto Iyengar. 1993. *The Media Game*. New York: Macmillan Publishing Company.

Best, Gary Dean. 1993. *The Critical Press and the New Deal: The Press versus Presidential Power, 1933–1938*. Westport, CT: Praeger Press.

Boorstin, Daniel. 1961. *The Image: A Guide to Pseudo-Events in America*. New York: Harper Colophon Books.

Braden, Waldo W. 1987. "Abraham Lincoln: Sixteenth President of the United States." In Bernard K. Duffy and Harford B. Ryan (Eds.) *American Orators Before 1900: Critical Studies and Sources*. Westport, CT: Greenwood Press.

Brand, H. W. 1998. *TR: The Last Romantic*. New York: Basic Books.

Broder, David, Lou Cannon, Haynes Johnson, Martin Schram, Richard Harwood, and the staff of the *Washington Post*. 1980. *The Pursuit of the Presidency*. New York: Berkley Publishing Company.

Brownlow, Louis. 1969. "What We Expect the President to Do." In Aaron Wildavsky (Ed.) *The Presidency*. Boston: Little, Brown and Company: 35–43.

Buchanan, Bruce. 1978. *The Presidential Experience: What the Office Does to the Man*. Englewood Cliffs, NJ: Prentice-Hall.

Buchanan, Bruce. 1995. "The Presidency and the Nominating Process." In Michael Nealon (Ed.),*The Presidency and the Political System*. Washington, D.C.: Congressional Quarterly Press.

Burns, James MacGregor. 1965. *Presidential Government: The Crucible of Leadership*. Boston: Houghton Mifflin.

Burns, James MacGregor. 1984. *Roosevelt: The Lion and the Fox*. New York: Harcourt, Brace, Jovanovich Publishers.

Cannon, Lou. 1991. *President Reagan: The Role of a Lifetime*. New York: Simon and Schuster.

Carter, Jimmy. 1982. *Keeping Faith: Memoirs of a President*. New York: Bantam Books.

Cronin, Thomas E. 1974. "The Textbook Presidency and Political Science." In Stanley Bach and George T. Sulzner (Eds.) *Perspectives on the Presidency*. Lexington, MA: D. C. Heath.

Cronin, Thomas E. 1977. "The Presidency and Its Paradoxes." In Thomas E. Cronin and Rexford G. Tugwell (Eds.) *The Presidency Reappraised*. New York: Praeger Publishers: 69–85.

Cronin, Thomas E. 1980. "Looking for Leadership, 1980." *Public Opinion Quarterly.* (February-March): 15.

Davis, Richard. 1996. *The Press and American Politics: The New Mediator.* Upper Saddle River, NJ: Prentice-Hall, Inc.

Deaver, Michael K. 1987. *Behind the Scenes.* New York: William Morrow and Company.

Degregorio, William A. 1991. *The Complete Book of U.S. Presidents.* New York: Wings Books.

DiClerico, Robert E. 1993. "The Role of the Media in Heightened Expectations and Diminished Leadership Capacity." In Richard W. Waterman (Ed.) *The Presidency Reconsidered.* Itasca, IL: Peacock Press: 115–143.

Donald, David Herbert. 1995. *Lincoln.* New York: Simon and Schuster.

Duffy, Michael and Dan Goodgame. 1992. *Marching in Place: The Status Quo Presidency of George Bush.* New York: Simon and Schuster.

Edel, Wilbur. 1992. *The Reagan Presidency: An Actor's Finest Performance.* New York: Hippocrene Books.

Edwards, George C. III. 1983. *The Public Presidency: The Pursuit of Popular Support.* New York: St. Martin's Press.

Edwards, George C. III and Stephen Wayne. 1997. *Presidential Leadership: Politics and Policy Making.* New York: St. Martin's Press.

Ehrlichman, John. 1982. *Witness to Power: The Nixon Years.* New York: Pocket Books.

Ellis, Joseph J. 1997. *American Sphinx: The Character of Thomas Jefferson.* New York: Alfred A. Knopf.

Finer, Herman. 1960. *The Presidency: Crisis and Regeneration.* Chicago: University of Chicago Press.

Fitzwater, Marlin. 1995. *Call the Briefing! Reagan and Bush, Sam and Helen: A Decade with Presidents and the Press.* New York: Random House.

Gallagher, Hugh Gregory. 1985. *FDR's Splendid Deception.* New York: Dodd, Mead, and Co.

Gant, Michael and Lilliard Richardson. 1993. "Presidential Performance, the Expectations Gap, and Negative Voter Support." In Richard Waterman (Ed.) *The Presidency Reconsidered.* Itasca, IL: F. E. Peacock Publishers.

Gelderman, Carol. 1997. *All the Presidents' Words: The Bully Pulpit and the Creation of the Virtual Presidency.* New York: Walker and Company.

Genovese, Michael A. 1995. *The Presidential Dilemma: Leadership in the American System.* New York: HarperCollins.

Germond, Jack W. and Jules Witcover. 1989. *Whose Broad Stripes and Bright Stars: The Trivial Pursuit of the Presidency 1988.* New York: Warner Books.

Goldman, Peter, Thomas M. DeFrank, Mark Miller, Andrew Murr, and Tom Mathews. 1994. *Quest for the Presidency 1992.* College Station, TX: Texas A and M University.

Goodwin, Doris Kearns. 1994. *No Ordinary Time: Franklin and Eleanor Roosevelt: The Home Front in World War II.* New York: Simon and Schuster.

Greenstein, Fred I. 1982. *The Hidden-Hand Presidency: Eisenhower as Leader.* New York: Basic Books.

Greenstein, Fred I. 1988. "Nine Presidents in Search of a Modern Presidency." In Fred I. Greenstein (Ed.) *Leadership in the Modern Presidency.* Cambridge, MA: Harvard University Press: 296–352.

Grossman, Michael Baruch and Martha Joynt Kumar. 1981. *Portraying the President: The White House and the News Media.* Baltimore: John Hopkins University Press.

Haldeman, H. R. with Joseph DiMona. 1978. *The Ends of Power.* New York: Times Books.

Haldeman, H. R. 1994. *The Haldeman Diaries: Inside the Nixon White House.* New York: G. P. Putnam's Sons.

Hamby, Alonzo L. 1995. *Man of the People: A Life of Harry S. Truman.* New York: Oxford University Press.

Hart, Roderick P. 1987. *The Sound of Leadership: Presidential Communication in the Modern Age.* Chicago: The University of Chicago Press.

Hersh, Seymour M. 1997. *The Dark Side of Camelot.* Boston: Little, Brown and Co.

Hinckley, Barbara. 1985. *Problems of the Presidency: A Text with Readings.* Glenview, IL: Scott, Foresman and Co.

Hinckley, Barbara. 1990. *The Symbolic Presidency: How Presidents Portray Themselves.* New York: Routledge Press.

Kerbel, Matthew Robert. 1995. *Remote and Controlled: Media Politics in a Cynical Age.* Boulder, CO: Westview Press, Inc.

Kernell, Samuel. 1985. "Campaigning, Governing, and the Contemporary Presidency." In John E. Chubb and Paul E. Peterson (Eds.) *The New Direction in American Politics.* Washington, D.C.: The Brookings Institution: 117–141.

Kernell, Samuel. 1997. *Going Public: New Strategies for Presidential Leadership.* Washington, D.C.: Congressional Quarterly Press.

Kimball, David C. and Samuel C. Patterson. 1997. "Living Up to Expectations: Public Attitudes Toward Congress." *Journal of Politics.* 59: 701–728.

Kimball, Warren F. 1991. *The Juggler: Franklin Roosevelt as Wartime Statesman.* Princeton: Princeton University Press.

Kinder, Donald R. 1986. "Presidential Character Revisited." In Richard R. Lau and David O. Sears (Eds.) *Political Cognition: The 19th Annual Carnegie Symposium.* Hillsdale, NJ: L. Erlbaum.

King, Gary and Lyn Ragsdale. 1988. *The Elusive Executive: Discovering Statistical Patterns in the Presidency.* Washington, D.C.: Congressional Quarterly Press.

Kolb, Charles. 1994. *White House Daze: The Unmaking of Domestic Policy in the Bush Years.* New York: The Free Press.

Kurtz, Howard. 1998. *Spin Cycle.* New York: The Free Press.

Kutler, Stanley I. 1997. *Abuse of Power: The New Nixon Tapes.* New York: The Free Press.

Leuchtenburg, William E. 1963. *Franklin D. Roosevelt and the New Deal.* New York: Harper & Row.

Light, Paul C. 1983. *The President's Agenda: Domestic Policy Choice from Kennedy to Carter.* Baltimore: John Hopkins University Press.

Lowi, Theodore J. 1985. *The Personal President: Power Invested Power Unfulfilled.* Ithaca, NY: Cornell University Press.

May, Ernest R. and Philip D. Zelikow. 1997. *The Kennedy Tapes: Inside the White House During the Cuban Missile Crisis.* Cambridge, MA: Harvard University Press.

Mayer, Jane and Doyle McManus. 1988. *Landslide: The Unmaking of the President 1984–1988.* Boston: Houghton Mifflin.

McCoy, Donald R. 1988. *Calvin Coolidge: The Quiet President.* Lawrence, KS: University Press of Kansas.

McCullough, David. 1992. *Truman.* New York: Simon and Schuster.

MCCullough, David. 1977. *The Path Between the Seas: The Creation of the Panama Canal 1870–1914.* New York: Simon and Schuster.

McGinniss, Joe. 1970. *The Selling of the President 1968.* New York: Pocket Books.

Michaels, Judith E. 1997. *The President's Call: Executive Leadership from FDR to George Bush.* Pittsburgh: University of Pittsburgh Press.

Milkis, Sidney M. and Michael Nelson. 1994. *The American Presidency: Origins & Development.* Washington, D.C.: Congressional Quarterly Press.

Miller, Nathan. 1992. *Theodore Roosevelt: A Life.* New York: William Morrow and Co.

Miroff, Bruce. 1988. "The Presidency and the Public: Leadership as Spectacle." In Michael Nelson (Ed.) *The Presidency and the Political System.* Washington, D.C.: Congressional Quarterly Press: 271–291.

Mitgang, Herbert (Ed.). 1989. *Abraham Lincoln: A Press Portrait.* Athens: The University of Georgia Press.

Moe, Terry. 1985. "The Politicized Presidency." In John E. Chubb and Paul E. Peterson (Eds.) *The New Direction in American Politics.* Washington, D.C.: The Brookings Institution: 235–271.

Morris, Dick. 1997. *Behind the Oval Office: Winning the Presidency in the Nineties.* New York: Random House.

Nelson, Michael. 1988. "Evaluating the Presidency." In Michael Nelson (Ed.) *The Presidency and the Political System.* Washington, D.C.: Congressional Quarterly Press: 5–28.

Neustadt, Richard E. 1980. *Presidential Power: The Politics of Leadership from FDR to Carter.* New York: John Wiley and Sons.

Nixon, Richard M. 1978. *RN: The Memoirs of Richard Nixon.* New York: Grosset & Dunlap.

Noonan, Peggy. 1990. *What I Saw at the Revolution: A Political Life in the Reagan Era.* New York: Random House.

Oates, Stephen B. 1984. *Abraham Lincoln: The Man Behind the Myths.* New York: New American Library.

Raichur, Arvind and Richard W. Waterman. 1993. "The Presidency, the Public and the Expectations Gap." In Richard W. Waterman (Ed.) *The Presidency Reconsidered.* Itasca, IL: F. E. Peacock Publishers: 1–21.

Reagan, Ronald. 1990. *An American Life.* New York: Simon and Schuster.

Reeves, Richard. 1993. *President Kennedy: Profile of Power.* New York: Simon and Schuster.

Regan, Donald T. 1988. *For the Record: From Wall Street to Washington.* New York: Harcourt, Brace, Jovanovich Publishers.

Reich, Robert. 1997. *Locked in the Cabinet.* New York: Alfred A. Knopf.

Riccards, Michael P. 1995. *The Ferocious Engine of Democracy: A History of the American Presidency.* Volumes 1 and 2. New York: Madison Books.

Robinson, Donald L. 1987. *To the Best of My Ability: The Presidency and the Constitution.* New York: W. W. Norton.

Rollins, Ed with Tom Defrank. 1996. *Bare Knuckles and Back Rooms: My Life in American Politics.* New York: Broadway Books.

Roosevelt, Theodore. 1985. *Theodore Roosevelt: An Autobiography.* New York: De Capo Press.

Rose, Gary L. 1997. *The American Presidency Under Siege.* Albany: State University of New York Press.

Rose, Richard. 1988. *The Postmodern Presidency: The White House Meets the World.* Chatham, NJ: Chatham House Publishers.

Rossiter, Clinton. 1960. *The American Presidency.* New York: Harcourt, Brace and World.

Rusk, Jerrold. 1987. "Issues and Voting." In S. Long (Ed.) *Research in Micro Politics: Voting Behavior.* Volume 2. Greenwich, CT: J.A.I. Press.

Schieffer, Bob and Gary Paul Gates. 1989. *The Acting President.* New York: E. P. Dutton.

Schlesinger, Arthur M. Jr. 1945. *The Age of Jackson.* Boston: Little, Brown and Company.

Schlesinger, Arthur M. Jr. (Ed.). 1994. *Running for President: The Candidates and Their Images 1789–1896.* Volumes 1 and 2. New York: Simon and Schuster.

Schwartz, Barry. 1987. *George Washington: The Making of an American Symbol.* New York: The Free Press.

Seligman, Lester G. and Michael Baer. 1969. "Expectations of Presidential Leadership in Decision-Making." In Aaron Wildavsky (Ed.) *The Presidency.* Boston: Little, Brown and Company: 18–35.

Seligman, Lester G. and Cary R. Covington. 1989. *The Coalitional Presidency.* Chicago: Dorsey Press.

Sharp, James Roger. 1993. *American Politics in the Early Republic: The New Nation in Crisis.* New Haven, CT: Yale University Press.

Skowronek, Stephen. 1993. *The Politics Presidents Make: Leadership From John Adams to George Bush.* Cambridge, MA: Belknap Press of Harvard University.

Speakes, Larry with Robert Pack. 1988. *Speaking Out: Inside the Reagan White House.* New York: Charles Scribner and Sons.

Stimson, James A. 1976. "Public Support for American Presidents: A Cyclical Model." *Public Opinion Quarterly* 40 (Spring): 1–21.

Stimson, James A. 1976-1977. "On Disillusionment with the Expectation/Disillusion Theory: A Rejoinder." *Public Opinion Quarterly* 40 (Winter): 541–543.

Stuckey, Mary E. 1991. *The President as Interpreter-in-Chief.* Chatham, NJ: Chatham House Publishers.

Sundquist, James L. 1981. *The Decline and Resurgence of Congress.* Washington, D.C.: Brookings Institution.

Tebbel, John and Sarah Miles Watts. 1985. *The Press and the Presidency: From George Washington to Ronald Reagan.* New York: Oxford University Press.

Thach, Charles C. Jr. 1969. *The Creation of the Presidency, 1775–1789: A Study in Constitutional History.* Baltimore: John Hopkins University Press.

Thomas, Norman C. and Joseph A. Pika, and Richard Watson. 1994 and 1997 editions. *The Politics of the Presidency.* Washington, D.C.: Congressional Quarterly Press.

Tufte, Edward R. 1978. *Political Control of the Economy.* Princeton: Princeton University Press.

Tulis, Jeffrey K. 1987. *The Rhetorical Presidency.* Princeton: Princeton University Press.

Waterman, Richard W. 1993. "Closing the Expectations Gap: The Presidential Search for New Political Resources." In Richard W. Waterman (Ed.) *The Presidency Reconsidered.* Itasca, IL: F. E. Peacock Publishers: 22–46.

Waterman, Richard W. 1996. "Storm Clouds on the Political Horizon: George Bush at the Dawn of the 1992 Presidential Election." *Presidential Studies Quarterly.* (Spring): 337–49.

Waterman, Richard W., Hank C. Jenkins-Smith, and Carol Silva. Forthcoming. "The Expectations Gap Thesis: Public Attitudes Toward an Incumbent President." *The Journal of Politics.*

Ward, John William. 1955. *Andrew Jackson: Symbol for an Age.* New York: Oxford University Press.

Wayne, Stephen J. 1982. "Great Expectations: What People Want from Presidents." In Thomas E. Cronin (Ed.) *Rethinking the Presidency.* Boston: Little, Brown and Company: 185–199.

Wilson, James Q. 1989. *Bureaucracy: What Government Agencies Do and Why They Do It.* New York: Basic Books.

Wilson, Woodrow. 1981. *Constitutional Government in the United States.* New York: Columbia University Press. (Original date of publication, 1885.)

Witcover, Jules. 1977. *Marathon: The Pursuit of the Presidency, 1972–1976.* New York: Viking Press.

White, Theodore. 1961. *The Making of the President 1960.* New York: New American Library.

Zaller, John R. 1998. "Monica Lewinsky's Contribution to Political Science." *PS: Political Science and Politics.* Vol XXXI No 2 (June): 182–189.

Index

Printed in the United States
102912LV00003B/212/A

9 780813 368924